Second Punic War 217–206 BC

Roman Legionary
VERSUS
Carthaginian Warrior

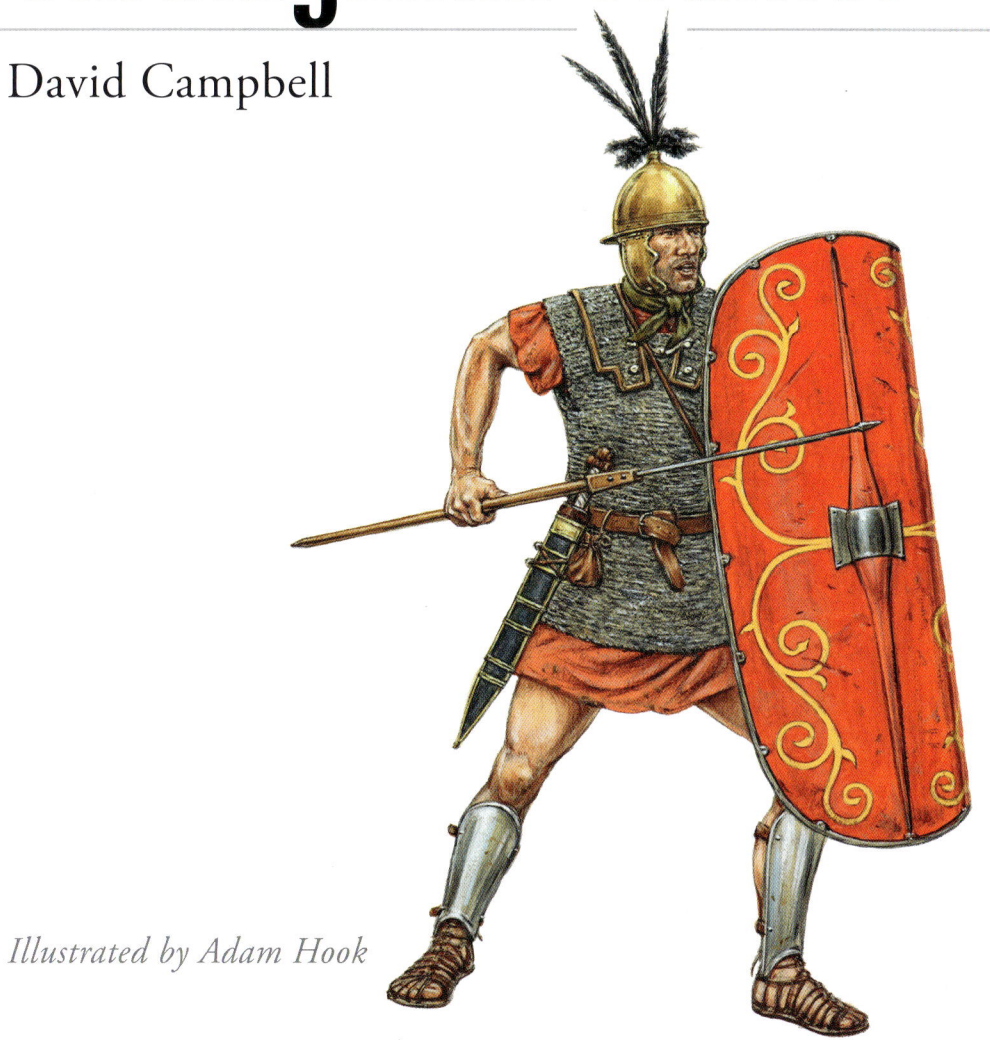

David Campbell

Illustrated by Adam Hook

OSPREY PUBLISHING
Bloomsbury Publishing Plc
PO Box 883, Oxford, OX1 9PL, UK
1385 Broadway, 5th Floor, New York, NY 10018, USA
E-mail: info@ospreypublishing.com
www.ospreypublishing.com

OSPREY is a trademark of Osprey Publishing Ltd

First published in Great Britain in 2018

© Osprey Publishing Ltd, 2018

All rights reserved. No part of this publication may be reproduced or transmitted in any form or by any means, electronic or mechanical, including photocopying, recording, or any information storage or retrieval system, without prior permission in writing from the publishers.

A catalogue record for this book is available from the British Library.

ISBN: PB 9781472828040; eBook 9781472828057;
ePDF 9781472828064; XML 9781472828071

18 19 20 21 22   10 9 8 7 6 5 4 3 2 1

Maps by bounford.com
Index by Rob Munro
Typeset by PDQ Digital Media Solutions, Bungay, UK
Printed in China through World Print Ltd.

Osprey Publishing supports the Woodland Trust, the UK's leading woodland conservation charity. Between 2014 and 2018 our donations are being spent on their Centenary Woods project in the UK.

To find out more about our authors and books visit www.ospreypublishing.com. Here you will find extracts, author interviews, details of forthcoming events and the option to sign up for our newsletter.

Dedication
To my godson Lucas McLean, who would really only be impressed by this dedication if it came at the front of a book about Judge Dredd.

Acknowledgements
I would like to thank: Mike Loades and Kim Hawkins for their kind provision of several images as well as the sharing of knowledge of ancient slinging; Kevin P. O'Connell for his research into the location of the battlefield of Ilipa; Marje and Vincent van Bijnen (www.the-romans.eu) for their kind permission to use a photograph of the battlefield of Ilipa; the Metropolitan Museum of Art of New York (www.metmuseum.org) for actively encouraging the use of their images in the interests of public education; the staff of Southsea Library for their patience in the face of my slovenly return of inter-library loans; Graham Campbell, whose relentless pursuit of home improvement has given me a better place to write; Geoff Banks for reminding us all of the value of shame; Mr Brian McCreesh and Mr Ron Forshaw, who did the best they could with the materials they had to hand; and Nick Reynolds at Osprey for knocking it all together, as always.

Editor's note
Citations of classical texts follow the usual practice (i.e. book volume, chapter, sub-chapter). Unless otherwise stated, all such citations refer to the books listed in the 'Classical Works' section of the bibliography.

Artist's note
Readers may care to note that the original paintings from which the colour plates in this book were prepared are available for private sale. All reproduction copyright whatsoever is retained by the publishers. All enquiries should be addressed to:

Scorpio, 158 Mill Road, Hailsham, East Sussex BN27 2SH, UK
Email: scorpiopaintings@btinternet.com

The publishers regret that they can enter into no correspondence upon this matter.

CONTENTS

INTRODUCTION	4
THE OPPOSING SIDES	8
Army formation • Infantry • Cavalry • Morale • Leadership and command	
LAKE TRASIMENE	29
June 217 BC	
CANNAE	41
Summer 216 BC	
ILIPA	57
206 BC	
ANALYSIS	72
Lake Trasimene • Cannae • Ilipa	
AFTERMATH	76
BIBLIOGRAPHY	78
INDEX	80

Introduction

On the eve of the first major encounter between Roman and Carthaginian troops in the Second Punic War, Hannibal drew his army around to watch a single combat, a fight to the death between a pair of Gauls chosen by lot from among those who had had the misfortune to be captured during his army's advance through the alpine passes. For the winner there would be horses, fine cloaks, armour and weapons as well as a place in Hannibal's army, for the loser the consolation of death, an escape preferable to the harsh servitude under which all the young Gauls had been labouring. Freed from their shackles and

Ancient ropes and wood are discovered at a Carthaginian shipwreck off the coast of Sicily. Punic naval supremacy was the key to the Carthaginian empire's reach and power, allowing it to dominate the whole of the western Mediterranean with its merchant vessels and warships, a state of affairs that would be overturned by the Romans in the First Punic War at the battle of the Aegates in 241 BC. Though engagements at sea would play a minor role in the Second Punic War, the real impact of continuing Roman naval supremacy was to force the Carthaginians into land-locked campaigns, abandoning strategies that relied on seaborne transport or supply. (Photo by Jonathan S. Blair/National Geographic/Getty Images)

FAR LEFT
A Carthaginian coin depicting an elephant, from Spain, 237–206 BC. Though Hannibal's elephants have seized the imagination of writers and artists down to the present day, they were a mixed blessing on the battlefield. The Carthaginian elephants are assumed to have been the now-extinct North African variety (distinct from the African Bush elephant and African Forest elephant), with Polybius noting their relatively small size in comparison to Asian elephants. In battle their main value was as a shock element that would disrupt enemy lines by causing panic and charging through tightly packed ranks of legionaries, which they certainly did on occasion. They were an unpredictable resource, however, causing more havoc for the Carthaginians than the Romans at the battle of Zama in 202 BC, for example, and the fact that the Romans never developed their own version of elephantine cavalry suggests that their tactical value lay more in the threat than the execution. (DEA/G. DAGLI ORTI/ De Agostini/Getty Images)

LEFT
A *denarius* bearing the image of Scipio Africanus, 2nd century BC. The reputations of both Scipio and especially Hannibal would far outlive their own day, with later ages finding much to admire and emulate in the deeds of their ancestors. Their battles and campaigns would become tactical touchstones for future generations of military men, but their impact was also cultural, both men being viewed as paragons of leadership and virtue according to the particular needs of their inheritors. (DEA/D. DAGLI ORTI/ De Agostini/Getty Images)

given fine weapons and mail coats, the two warriors set about one another, fighting until one fell; the remaining Gauls congratulated the victor, but also the dead man on his freedom from any further woes, a sentiment that was echoed by the watching throng of Carthaginian troops. At this point Hannibal came forward and explained that the fight they had just witnessed was an example of the fate that awaited them all: they too could conquer, and the unimagined wealth of Rome would be theirs, or they could die fighting, knowing that they gave their lives in a noble cause. The only other option was to try to flee, but where they now stood, in the shadow of a Roman army, there could be no successful escape, so far away were they from their homelands; those who sought to save their own lives would be damned to live as prisoners and slaves. Only by giving themselves up to the alternatives of an honourable death or glorious victory would they have the necessary strength to overcome such a formidable foe in his own lands (Polybius 3.63).

Such was the mind-set of the Carthaginian army at the outset of the Second Punic War in 218 BC. The uncompromising nature of Hannibal's words was a sign of the deep enmity that burned between Carthage and Rome, a fierce and driven antagonism that had fuelled both powers in the First Punic War (264–241 BC), a ferocious battle for supremacy that lasted for a generation and left the Romans victorious. Defeated on land and broken at sea, the Carthaginians had been punished by losing the war, then again in having to endure a humiliating peace that saw them surrendering vast treasures in tribute. The fires that had burned so bright during the war were not extinguished by such a peace, the embers continuing to glow until the opportunity came to fan them back to life.

The Western Mediterranean, 218–206 BC

MAP KEY

Rome and Carthage had already fought the First Punic War over the possession of Sicily (264–241 BC), a conflict Carthage lost, being forced to withdraw from the island and pay an indemnity of 1,000 talents of gold immediately and a further 2,200 talents over the following ten years (a Roman talent weighed 32.3kg). That failure provoked a domestic rebellion known as the Mercenary War (240–238 BC), this time with the loss of Sardinia and Corsica as the price, again to Rome, though the Romans were not belligerents in the war – more avaricious bystanders who made the most of their neighbour's misfortunes, an insult that was further compounded by the Roman demand for another 1,200 talents to boot.

One brief glimmer of hope for Carthage came from the accomplishments of its native son Hamilcar Barca, who had succeeded in quelling the revolt. His success became a stepping stone to an expedition from Carthage to Iberia led by Hamilcar, the object being to rebuild the fortunes of the mother city that had been so sadly diminished by the war with Rome. Hamilcar arrived in the old Phoenician city of Gades (Cádiz) in 237 BC intent on 're-establishing the Carthaginians' affairs in Iberia' (Polybius 2.1.6), which he set about doing with a vengeance, pacifying large areas dominated by warlike tribes and developing the silver mines of the Sierra Morena mountains. The violent expansion of 'Carthaginian affairs' was as much an expansion of the Barcid family's influence and power as it was a state-driven enterprise, perhaps even more so; it certainly would benefit Hannibal when he came into his inheritance at the age of 26 in 221 BC, continuing the subjugation of the tribal peoples of Iberia that had been started by his father, expanding his fiefdom in a series of impressive campaigns around the country. The difference with Hannibal was that his efforts to strengthen Carthage (and his own power) had a definite end in mind – to generate the money and manpower needed to allow him to make war upon Rome.

Hannibal, inheritor of his family's army in Iberia, had made the most of his time in that province, a land rich in silver and warlike tribes. The men of his army trusted him 'because he seemed to have great aptitude and fondness for war' (Appian 7.1.3), something he demonstrated in the spring of 219 BC by laying siege to Saguntum, an Iberian coastal town under the protection of Rome, taking it after eight months. Naturally outraged at such an act, Rome blustered, demanding Hannibal's head from Carthage if they wished to avoid another war. As Hannibal was at that very moment making his preparations to invade Italia, such an ultimatum fell on deaf ears.

A republic with elected leaders and an enfranchised, engaged citizenry, the city that Hannibal sought to conquer was a nascent empire in all but name. Through battle and bloodshed Rome had spread its authority over all its neighbouring lands, eventually controlling the whole of Italia through a series of alliances that fed money and men into its army, the ever-hungry tool of its expansion. The first war against Carthage had set the seal on Roman ascendancy outside Italia, and even without Hannibal's provocation at Saguntum another war with the Carthaginians was likely unavoidable when their interests collided once again, as they inevitably would. For Hannibal the aim was to bring the war home to the Romans, to drive deep into their heartlands, defeat their armies, make a mockery of their claims to power and fracture their carefully nurtured network of alliances, leaving Rome stripped bare and at his mercy. He would come to learn that though he could breach their borders, lay waste to lands the length and breadth of the country, and not just defeat but annihilate their armies in battle after battle, they would not yield. Hannibal certainly understood war, practising it as few others before him had, but he did not understand Rome, and that misapprehension would cost him – and Carthage – dearly.

Galli
GAUL
PYRENEES
Numantia
Celtiberi
Lusitani
IBERIA
Saguntum
BALEARIC ISLANDS
Iberi
Baecula
Ilipa
Baetis
New Carthage
Gades
Masaesylii
Numidi
Massylii (Maesulii)
Carthage
Tunis
Rhône
Massilia
Liguri
Genua
ALPS
Ticinus
Insubres
Trebia
Boii
APENNINES
Padus
Ariminum
Senones
ILLYRIA
Adriatic Sea
(Mare Adriaticum)
Lake Trasimene
Tiber
Rome
Cannae
CORSICA
SARDINIA
Tyrrhenian Sea
(Mare Tyrrhenum)
Mediterranean Sea
SICILY
Syracuse
N
0
250 miles
0
250km

The Opposing Sides

ARMY FORMATION

Roman

The Roman army of the mid-Republican period was not, strictly speaking, a professional force; rather it was made up from a *legio* (levy) of citizens who passed requirements of age (between 17 and 49 years) and property (to the value of or above 11,000 *assēs*, an *as* being a bronze, later copper coin, ten of which were worth one silver *denarius*). Despite this civic foundation, the men who found themselves as legionaries would have almost certainly undergone much in the way of martial training during their early years, either from militaristic activities such as hunting or directly as part of their education within their families, for whom the bearing and use of arms was a primary duty of manhood. When a man fought for Rome he was not just fulfilling his duty to the state, he was also demonstrating his responsibilities as a citizen as well as fighting for his own home and prospects in a very practical sense.

The development of Roman civic life and institutions in the period up to and during the Punic Wars was reflected in the army, and certainly by the time of the war against Hannibal the city's military culture was not so much a facet of Roman society as it was an expression of it. The broad basis of the men who served, the fact that their officers on campaign were the same men that they had elected at home, the ethos of their life within the legions, the development of a regular and repeatable system of supply and camp-building – all bespoke an army that was becoming indivisible from the state that employed it. The hallmarks of such a force were discipline and training, with Romans developing professional attitudes to warfare long before the army had professional institutions (Keppie 1984: 55), a process that was much accelerated by the intense battles against Hannibal. Such an army may have had its origins in a civic militia but it had evolved into a radically different

A Roman fresco representing a Campanian hoplite, 6th century BC. The old Roman hoplite army of the 5th century BC was first and foremost a political institution that performed various tasks of self-defence with reasonable efficiency in much the same manner as its neighbours did. The practice of Roman arms underwent significant change throughout the 4th century BC, however: the state evolved to be more responsive to the needs of its citizens, allowing greater participation in politics as well as a better share of war booty which in turn helped to light the expansionist aggression that would be such a hallmark of Rome in the following century. In the practice of warfare they grew into the habit of adopting weapons, armour and tactics that they knew to be effective (having been on the receiving end of them), for example the oblong shield from the Samnites, and an evolution towards relying more on the sword than the spear for close combat. By the time of the Punic Wars the tactics and methods of a Roman battle were distinctive and notably more effective than those of many of their opponents. (DEA PICTURE LIBRARY/De Agostini/Getty Images)

beast from the sorts of traditional armies fielded by contemporary Hellenistic states, with war becoming both the means and the ends to the men who served within it.

The Roman military establishment was based around a body of four standing legions with a commensurate number of allied troops, but this system underwent substantial increases throughout the Second Punic War (218–201 BC). In 218 BC Rome had raised six legions to meet the Carthaginian threat, a force that more than doubled to 14 in the wake of the losses at Lake Trasimene (217 BC) and Cannae (216 BC), eventually rising to a high of 25 legions in 212–211 BC. The average number of legions remained around 20 until 203–201 BC when the discharge of various units reduced the overall number to 14. Such numbers were probably matched by *alae* (allied legions), though in both Roman and allied cases it is impossible to say what the active strength of such legions was. Certainly after 200 BC the *supplementa* system seems to have ensured that most legions were kept at or near their full strength, but it is reasonable to assume that during the preceding period of warfare that lasted for an entire generation, such efficiency would not always have been possible (Brunt 2001: 417–22).

To augment its own soldiers, Rome relied on the *formula togatorum* ('rota of toga-wearers'), a list that detailed the military obligations that were owed by cities of the Latin League (the *nomen Latinum* or 'Latin name') and the *socii* (Italian 'allies'). During the Second Punic War it was usual for half a Roman force (sometimes more) to be made up of such troops, with each Roman legion being matched by an allied one. Though there is little direct evidence as to how they were armed or trained, the implication is that they were comparable to the Roman legions; it is likely that allied legions were trained, armed and organized in much the same way, if perhaps to a less

COMBAT Roman *princeps*

The legionary, a *princeps* of the second line, is around 30 years old and is a tried-and-tested veteran, having come through the disaster at the Trebia during the dying days of the previous year. As a man of some means he can afford fine armour and weapons, though all are somewhat worn with heavy use. The legionary himself is dusty and his tunic rather faded and dirty, as one might expect after some days of hard marching in pursuit of the elusive Carthaginians. He is moving aggressively towards his enemy, left foot forward, shield held high to protect his body and lower face, with his *pilum* at the ready for a killing thrust.

Lake Trasimene 217 BC

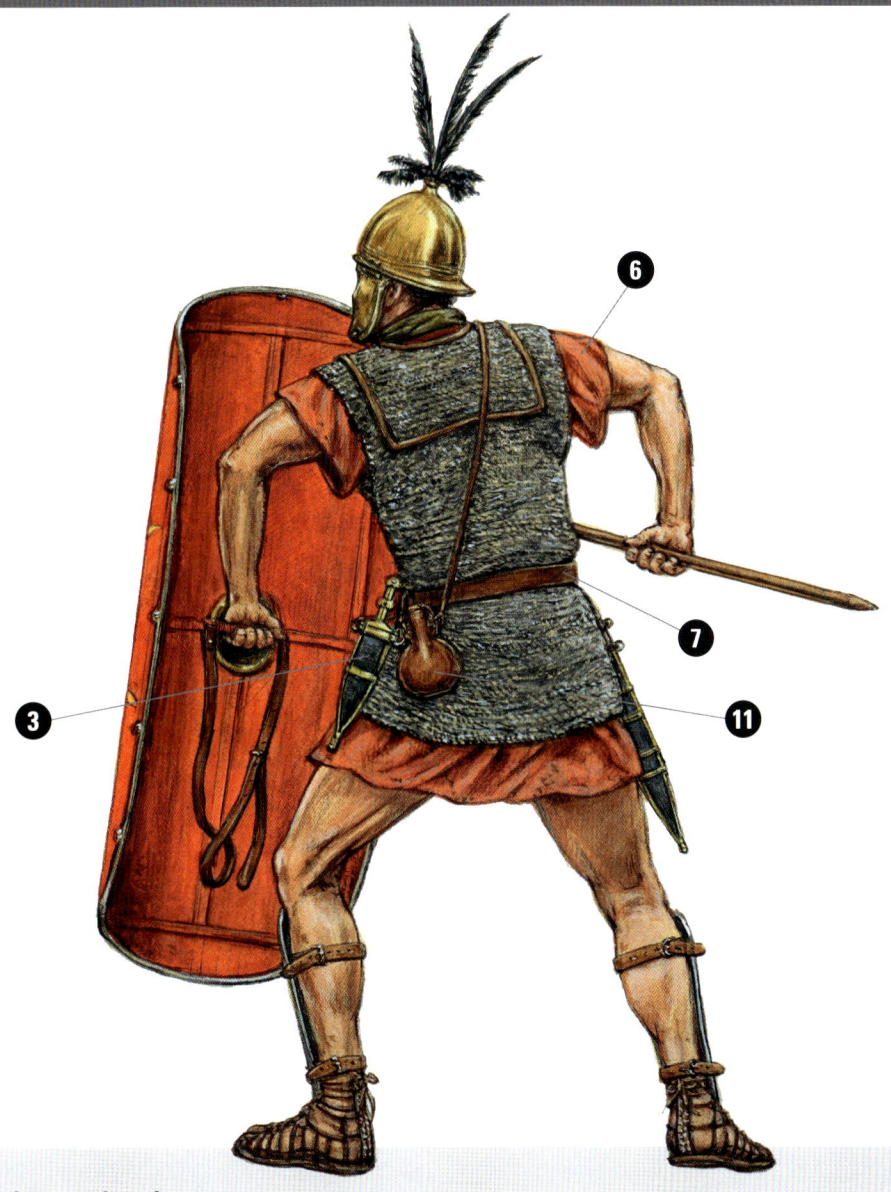

Weapons, dress and equipment

The legionary carries a *pilum* in his right hand (**1**) – based on examples found at the excavations of Ephyra in Greece and Castellruf in Spain – with a *gladius Hispaniensis* (**2**) belted to his right hip and a *pugio* (**3**) on his left hip. He wears a Montefortino-style helmet (**4**) with 'Olympia' style cheek-pieces and which sports a feather crest; as a wealthier citizen of Rome he is protected by a *lorica hamata* (**5**) with shoulder-doubling for added protection, worn over a *subarmalis* (a form of padded shirt to make the mail shirt more comfortable to wear) and a red linen tunic (**6**); though this colour is usually associated with Roman legionaries, there probably was not any consistent 'uniform' for legions during this period, especially considering that each soldier was responsible for the supply of his own clothing and equipment. The *lorica hamata* is cinched at the waist with a *cingulum* (a plain leather belt; **7**); as well as being the means for carrying his weapons, a legionary's belt was beneficial because it transferred some of the weight of the *lorica hamata* to the wearer's hips, reducing the burden on his shoulders (Bishop & Coulston 2006: 67). His shins are protected by a pair of greaves (**8**) – again a sign of wealth, as most *hastati* and *principes* would only have a single greave if they were lucky, worn on their 'dominant' left leg – and his feet are shod with *caligae* (hob-nailed boots; **9**), though their inclusion here is speculative as there is no evidence for when this footwear was adopted by the Roman army. He carries a coin purse on his belt (**10**), as well as a worn leather water bottle suspended from a thong slung over his shoulder (**11**). He carries the heavy curved *scutum* in his left hand (**12**). The total weight of his weapons, armour and equipment comes to around 26kg.

A line of re-enactors in *loricae hamatae*, their *gladii* at the ready. The process of transforming a young Roman into a man ready to stand in the legion began early. His father, uncles and older brothers would all likely have had extensive experience in war, creating a sea of stories and examples that would spur the young man's interest in warfare, likely augmented by the ownership and display of personal armour within the household, perhaps even trophies or awards for great deeds. Growing up in such an environment a boy would learn the martial values expected of him; he would see, handle and begin to train with the same sort of weapons and armour that he could one day expect to wear into battle himself. (DEA/C. BALOSSINI/ De Agostini/Getty Images)

exacting standard than for those raised by Rome proper, and thus they were well able to take their place in a force that was to campaign and fight in the Roman fashion.

Carthaginian

Carthage had been the dominant power of the western Mediterranean for centuries, its strength derived from trade across a broad maritime empire, an empire that was severely shaken and reduced as a result of Carthage's defeat in the First Punic War. In the wake of that disaster considerable efforts were expended in developing new territories and wealth in Iberia, actions that would have a considerable impact not just on the strategy of the Second Punic War but also on the composition and character of much of the Carthaginian army. Coming to definite conclusions about most aspects of the organization, composition and tactics of Hannibal's armies is fraught with difficulty and relies more on inference and assumption than one would like; archaeological evidence is scant, and textual observations derive almost entirely from Greek or Roman sources, all with their own agendas, some of them written at some considerable distance in time from the events they recall. Nevertheless, the impact such armies made on the Graeco-Roman world was substantial enough to ensure that even their enemies gave them their due.

Though Carthaginian power was still formidable during Hannibal's ascendancy, the city itself was nowhere near as populous as Rome, and its traditional focus had always been on the manning of its navy, so it had a much more restricted pool of manpower on which to call when it came to the raising of armies. The nature of Carthaginian society was oligarchic, as might be expected from a state whose power came from its wide-ranging mercantile endeavours, and the armies that it assembled had a similar quality, being drawn from different provinces and allied states, with treaty and payment being the primary method of securing the large numbers of men that were needed. Usually raised for a specific campaign, a Carthaginian army would have a small backbone of citizen soldiers significantly outnumbered by tributary levies from allies, as well as large mercenary contingents from warrior cultures such as the slingers of the Balearic Islands or the Celtiberians, the recruitment of whom would be facilitated by Carthage's extensive trading network. The chief sources of such troops were the tribes and societies of North Africa and the broad swathes of southern and central Iberia, all of which were underneath the Carthaginian heel (Fields 2010: 15–16). After Hannibal's crossing of the Alps considerable numbers of warlike Gaulish tribes would also be drawn to his banner through a blend of revenge and mercenary opportunity.

Once marshalled these heterogeneous forces would be commanded by Carthaginian officers, most of whom were likely drawn from the city's great families who often had generations of experience in raising armies and fighting them on campaigns throughout North Africa, Iberia and the Hellenistic world. Such a 'cultural unity' of command was important because of the disparate nature of the armies; made up from a patchwork of troop types, the contingents varied in size and skills, with different equipment and tactics as well. Organization was based on nationality, the structure of the mercenary contingent or allied levy remaining the same as when it was admitted to the army; no attempts were made to force these groups to adhere to predetermined

A relief depicting a phalanx, Thessaloniki, Greece. The use of the phalanx had dominated Greek and later Hellenistic warfare for centuries, and it continued to play an important role in Hannibal's armies, scoring some notable successes such as the envelopment of the Roman army flanks at Cannae. Despite such victories, Hannibal's use of the phalanx was different from those employed by Alexander, for example, in that his Libyo-Phoenician phalanges were only one part of a larger army that also employed a variety of other types of infantry and cavalry, all of whom were organized differently and employed their own particular tactics in battle. Homogeneity, one of the great strengths of a Hellenistic battle line, was nowhere to be found in Carthaginian armies. (DEA/G. DAGLI ORTI/ De Agostini/Getty Images)

COMBAT Iberian *scutarius*

This Iberian *scutarius* is a man of some standing, made evident by his wealth of arms and armour. As part of Hannibal's lure he and his fellow Iberians have endured the brunt of the Roman column's attack; he has been fighting hard, and it shows in his battered shield, rough appearance and several small cuts and scrapes to his arms and legs. Trying to stop the *extraordinarii* from breaking through he is rearing back in the act of casting his light spear, using his shield as a counterweight to impart more force to the throw.

Lake Trasimene 217 BC

Weapons, dress and equipment

The warrior is armed with a *hasta velitaris* (**1**), a Roman light javelin that proved to be very popular among the Romans' Punic enemies. He carries a falcata (**2**) suspended from a baldric – the falcata (likely derived from the very similar Greek *kopis*) was a fine weapon that excelled at slashing blows, but which could also be used for thrusting, – and a simple dagger (**3**). His broad leather belt (**4**) is a distinctive Iberian item. He is protected by a Celtic-influenced Montefortino-type helmet (**5**) with triple-disc cheek-pieces and a horsehair crest, as well as a mail shirt (**6**) worn over a leather *subarmalis* (**7**) and linen tunic; his legs are protected by a pair of greaves (**8**) and he carries an Iberian-pattern shield (**9**) decorated with a personal motif. His weapons and armour weigh around 20kg.

Bas-relief depicting a warrior from a memorial monument found in Urso (Osuna), southern Spain. The spined oval shield, broad belt and horse-head falcata are typical of the warriors of the late 3rd century BC, though the crested, apparently layered headgear he wears has been the subject of debate, some associating it with the description of caps made of sinew recounted by Strabo. The figure appears to wear only an embroidered tunic, with no other armour. (DEA / G. NIMATALLAH/De Agostini/Getty Images)

tactical divisions, or to adapt their ways of warmaking towards some abstract tactical principle (Daly 2002: 83). Each fought in the way they always had, with their own people by their side.

INFANTRY

Roman

The Roman legion of the Punic Wars was 4,500 men strong (4,200 infantry, 300 cavalry), having evolved from 4th-century versions that had followed the hoplite pattern of deploying the heavy foot soldiers in a single line of varying depth, towards the *triplex acies*, a system of three distinct lines – the *hastati*, *principes* and *triarii*. The main advantage of the *triplex acies* seems to have been the flexibility it offered the Romans in the replacement of weary troops with fresh men, enabling them to maintain the pressure on their enemy's more monolithic line as well as being better able to resist being worn down by his attacks (Sabin 2000: 7). The first line was made up of the *hastati* (1,200 per legion); the *hastatus* was a younger man armed with the *pilum* (heavy javelin)

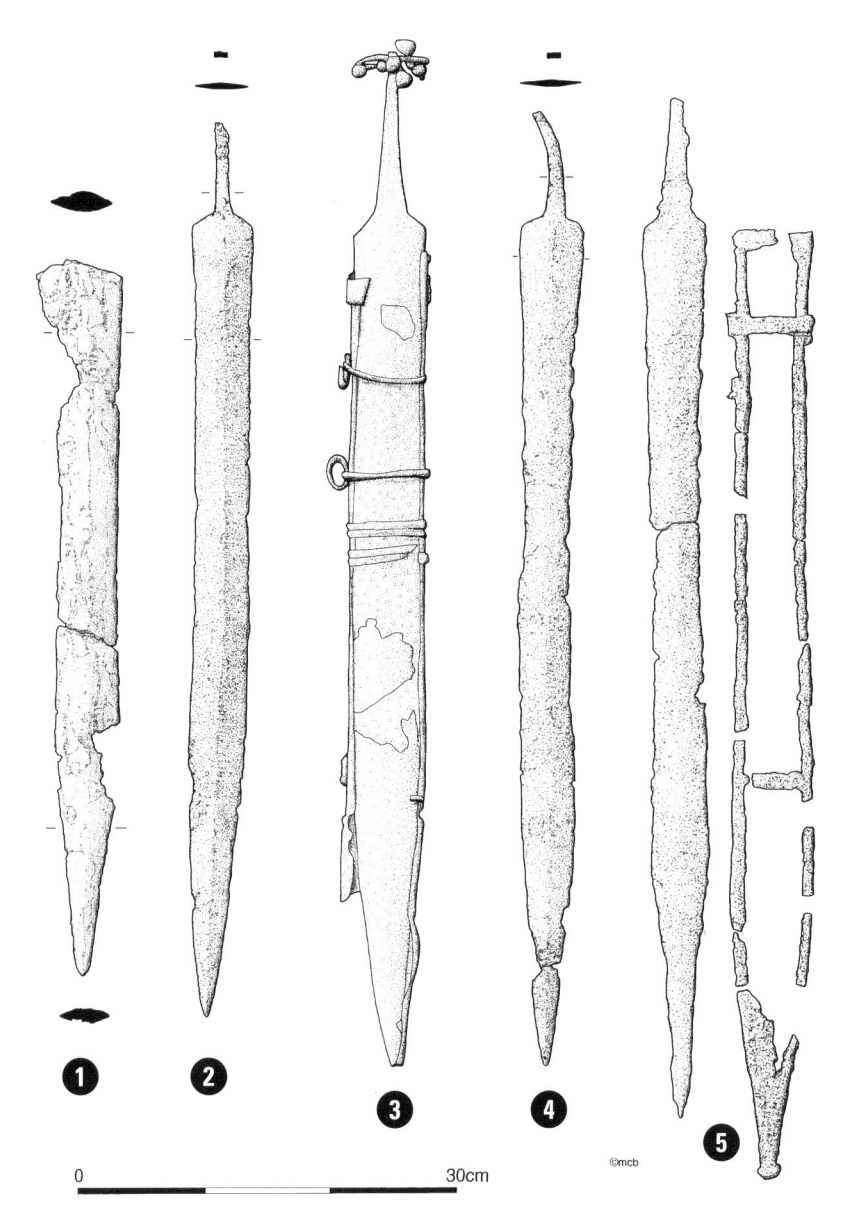

Developed from a design originating in Iberia, the *gladius* (a generic Latin term for a sword) was most likely adopted by the Roman army in the years after the First Punic War (Bishop 2016: 9–11). This drawing shows Republican *gladius Hispaniensis*-type swords from Alfaro in Spain (**1**), Šmihel in Slovenia (**2**, **4**), Delos in Greece (**3**) and Giubiasco in Switzerland (**5**). During the mid-Republican period the *gladius Hispaniensis* would be worn on the right hip by legionaries, attached to the wearer's belt and not worn on a baldric, as in later periods. Centurions used baldric-slung swords, but traditionally wore them on their left hip. There is little in the way of archaeological evidence to suggest the exact methods used by legionaries to attach swords to their belts, though as the sword was not a piece of issued equipment but rather the personal property of the individual who carried it, it seems reasonable to assume that there were a variety of methods of attachment depending on the design of a given sword's scabbard, as well as the preference of the wearer. (M.C. Bishop)

and *gladius* (short sword) and protected by a *scutum* (large shield), a helmet and bronze pectoral, with some men probably having greaves as well. The second line was made up of the *principes* (1,200 per legion); the *princeps* was typically a man in his prime armed and armoured in the same fashion as the *hastatus* but probably more likely to wear a *lorica hamata* (mail coat). The third line was made up of the *triarii* (600 per legion), older men with plenty of experience. The *triarius* would very likely wear a *lorica hamata* and was armed with a long *hasta* (spear). A legion would also have a contingent of light infantry – the *velites* (1,200 per legion) – who would form up as a loose screen ahead of the main force; the typical *veles* was probably unarmoured, wearing a simple helmet and carrying a light shield, armed with a handful of javelins and a *gladius*. A 300-strong cavalry element completed the legion.

RIGHT
The bent shank and point of a *pilum*, found at Cambodunum (Kempten), southern Germany. The *pilum*, like much of the Roman legionary's weapons and equipment, was adopted from his enemies, though exactly when and from which enemy is a matter of conjecture (for historians both ancient and modern); it seems most likely to have been adopted from either the Samnites or Iberians, but the textual and archaeological evidence is not definitive. (Xocolatl/Wikimedia/CC BY-SA 4.0)

FAR RIGHT
Replicas of Roman lead slingshot (*glandes plumbeae*, 'lead acorns'). Slingshot were manufactured from a variety of materials including shaped stone, clay and lead. Lead slingshot were often cast (in clay or stone moulds) in semi-industrial processes that produced numbers of bullets on a single sprue, often with symbols, monograms or words inscribed on them. Symbols used included lightning bolts, scorpions and bulls' heads, while those with monograms or words could refer to the name of a unit or its commander, personal names, civic locations, and jibes or insults such as 'greetings', 'take this' or 'ouch'. The markings on Roman *glandes* in particular tended to be provocative sexual taunts, in line with the conflation of military and sexual success that was common in Latin culture (Kelly 2012: 290–96). (Image courtesy of Mike Loades)

A crucial element in the effective employment of the *triplex acies* was the use of maniples. Literally meaning 'a handful', a maniple (*manipulus*) consisted of two centuries; a century (*centuria*) was 60 men strong. Each of the three main lines was broken down into ten maniples (120 men each for the *hastati* and *principes*, 60 men each for the *triarii*), each maniple being commanded by a centurion (*centurio*) with an *optio* acting as a junior officer. There is still much debate about the exact manner in which maniples were deployed, as well as the methods they used to manoeuvre during battle, but what does seem certain is that the maniple gave the Roman battle line much more tactical flexibility than that afforded to their enemies. The maniples of the three lines were spaced in a *quincunx* pattern (named after the pattern of five pips on the side of a die): the *hastati* would deploy with their maniples in line, spread out so that there was a maniple-sized space between each one; the *principes* would deploy behind them in the same fashion, but in such a way that their maniples covered the gaps left in the first line, and so on with the *triarii*. Such a system made it easier for other troops – cavalry or *velites*, for example – to filter through a Roman battle line, and it would make manoeuvring over rough or broken ground without losing cohesion a much more straightforward affair.

The nature of how a Roman battle line behaved as it approached that of an enemy has been the subject of some research by the historian Philip Sabin, who does not subscribe to the traditional view of ancient warfare (Sabin 1996). By most historical accounts the battles of the mid-Republican period (*c*.290 BC–88 BC) lasted for hours, and thus were unlikely to have been a constant clash of hand-to-hand combat into which succeeding lines of men were fed only to be hewn down by their apparently tireless enemies. Rather, he suggests that combat between two lines of infantry was dominated by pauses and lulls, both natural and deliberate, during which the two sides would pull back from one another to recuperate (or swap out exhausted maniples for fresh ones in the Roman case), the space between them filled by periodic surges led by more disciplined and aggressive elements of each force. Such assaults would involve short but intense bouts of close combat that would last until one side or the other sought to disengage, withdrawing to the safety of their main line, a practice that would occur all along the battle line in successive locally organized waves that would likely see one side being slowly pushed back by the other, something mentioned in the sources. Such a process would continue until one side's line began to fracture through localized stress or an overall loss of cohesion caused by the rolling attacks, the slow retreat suddenly turning into a rout that allowed the serious bloodletting to begin (Sabin 1996: 72). Such behaviour would certainly make sense in the light of Roman deployments of their three battle lines and manipular tactics, both of which could be seen as an attempt to manage the realities of ancient close combat between large bodies of organized troops.

Carthaginian

A distinct people that should not be confused with the citizens of Carthage, the Libyo-Phoenicians lived in towns and cities between the Atlantic coast of Modern Morocco (including a stretch of Iberia between Cádiz and Almería), through the coast of North Africa to the borders of Egypt (Salimbeti & D'Amato 2014: 17). They were at one remove from full Carthaginian citizens, and proved to be extremely useful as a source of manpower; Libyo-Phoenicians were most likely recruited through levy, and though some may have been light infantry the majority would have been armed and armoured in the Hellenistic fashion, with a helmet, cuirass (possibly of the linen *linothorax* type), greaves, shield, sword and probably a long *sarissa*-style spear. There is no agreement as to the type of spear used, its length, or the tactical formation employed by the Libyo-Phoenicians on the battlefield; the historian Gregory Daly, for example, believes it unlikely that Libyo-Phoenician troops operated in a traditional Greek phalanx, instead being heavy spearmen comparable to the Roman *hastati* and *principes* (Daly 2002: 86–90). They certainly re-equipped themselves (probably with *loricae hamatae*) from the dead at Trasimene, though the *pilum* and *scutum* would have required retraining to make them useful to their nascent owners, something that would be out of character for a Carthaginian army, so those items were probably ignored. Polybius described them as fighting in phalanxes at Cannae and elsewhere, and those formations may have been the Macedonian-style tactical unit (something that should not be dismissed – Polybius was trained and experienced in Hellenistic warfare) or a simple mass of spearmen, relying on weight of numbers. In the grand tactical scheme, however, it makes relatively little difference – they were heavy infantry.

The success of Carthage in bringing most of central and southern Iberia under its control was a crucial element in Hannibal's ability to prosecute his war against Rome, the peninsula offering him something like the manpower resources enjoyed by his enemy (Rawlings 1996: 81). Iberian levies probably

A reproduction of a seven-strand esparto grass Balearian sling with a stone bullet. Slingers carried three slings of various lengths – long for long distance, medium for medium distance and short for close range – and wore them as belts and headbands, for example, when not in use. Slingers would decide upon their target (probably an individual enemy soldier for a short sling, more likely a body of men for the longer slings) and then launch their projectiles in a single fluid motion. The damage that such stones and lead bullets (*glandes*) could do varied, depending on the strength and skill of the slinger, the distance to the target, the location of the impact on the body, and the armour (or lack of it) worn by the victim, but they could certainly penetrate skin, break bones and kill. (Image courtesy of Mike Loades)

A remarkably well-preserved Iberian falcata, likely 5th–1st centuries BC, with an (inaccurate) set of modern replacement wooden grips. The falcata (a 19th-century term coined by a Spanish antiquarian) was similar to (and likely developed from) the Greek *kopis* by way of the Celts, which it resembled in most particulars; it could be used for thrusting, but the pattern of its blade, dropping towards the point with a convex edge, lent itself to significant slashing and hacking blows. (Metropolitan Museum of Art, www.metmuseum.org)

fell into two rough classifications, the *scutarii* and the *caetrati*, determined by their type of shield (the *scutum* being a large flat oval shield with a wooden spine and metal boss, sometimes cut flat at the top and bottom, while the smaller and lighter *caetra* was flat and round with a circular metal boss). Both would be armed with a dagger and sword, the latter most likely a falcata type but also straight-bladed weapons similar to the *gladius Hispaniensis*, as well as spears for hand-to-hand fighting and for throwing. Helmets would have been of a variety of types, but most of the men would not have had any other armour (the better-off perhaps owning a bronze pectoral) The *scutarius* with his large and heavy shield would be a conventional infantryman, while the *caetratus* was a light infantryman, using his speed to dart forward and throw javelins at the enemy, fending off attacks with his light and manoeuvrable shield.

Known for their large stature, often terrifying appearance (their hair stiffened with limewash) and violent war cries both before and during battle, Gauls were an intimidating enemy. They had no regular formations, being divided by tribe and most likely operating in clans and family groups, perhaps 250 men strong (Connolly 1998: 187). Their tactics were rudimentary, consisting of a wild and violent charge that, if it failed to overwhelm on the first try, would often lose what little cohesion and impetus it had. Gauls were also perceived to lack endurance and suffer from brittle morale, fleeing the battlefield when things took a turn for the worse (Rawlings 1996: 87), though on an individual basis their courage and willingness to throw themselves on their enemy, driven by competition with one another as well as an intense sense of martial pride, made them a foe to be reckoned with.

As opposed to the Iberians, who were drawn from the central and southern parts of Iberia under Carthaginian control, the Celtiberians were from the north, and those of them who joined with Hannibal and his armies would likely have done so as mercenaries. In organization and military effectiveness they would have been much the same as the Gauls: fierce, independent and dangerous. The Balearians were mercenary slingers with a long association with Carthage going back to service before the First Punic War. Unlike other slingers, the Balearians used large stones in favour of lead bullets, and seem to have been one of Hannibal's more reliable units.

CAVALRY

Roman

There is no doubt that the cavalry contingent of a Roman army was important, its *turmae* (squadrons) being composed of some of the city's wealthiest and most ambitious young *equites* (horsemen), but it was hampered by its usually small size. Generals (such as Paullus and Varro at Cannae) rode with their cavalry, commanding their armies from the wings where such forces were traditionally deployed. Initially coming to the fore in the First Samnite War of 343–341 BC, probably under the influence of the Campanians who were noted horsemen, the Roman cavalry contingent was a recognized part of a legion's organization by the time of the Punic Wars. Each legion would field 300 men divided into ten *turmae* of 30 men each; each *turma* was led by a senior decurion (*decurio*) assisted by two more decurions, with three *optiones* acting as junior officers. A Roman cavalry contingent rarely comprised more than 10 per cent of an army's strength, and would often find itself overmatched when facing the larger numbers of Hannibal's more rough-and-ready horsemen from Iberia and North Africa.

Roman horsemen were probably armed and armoured in the Greek fashion, with helmet, cuirass (or mail coat), round or oval shield, spear and sword; owing to their good armour it is more likely that they would use their spears in hand-to-hand combat, as opposed to throwing them in the Numidian fashion. They were likely well-trained, and good riders too, even if not so naturally gifted as some of Hannibal's native horse contingents; though they were made up of mostly young aristocratic men the *equites* would have

A Celtic sword with a distinctive anthropomorphic grip, from the Tène culture, *c.*450 BC–AD 1. (Held in pantoffeln/Wikimedia/ CC BY-SA 4.0)

A reproduction of a Roman four-horn saddle. Used without stirrups, such a style of saddle would give a rider a very secure seat from which to engage foot soldiers or other riders. Roman cavalry were drawn from the highest social classes (primarily the *equites*, though later from the First Class as well), and as such they were expected to supply their own horses, weapons and equipment (in a similar, if more expensive manner, to the legionaries, though they would be reimbursed for the loss of a mount on campaign). Though there is little reliable evidence for the arms and equipment used by mid-Republican cavalry, the fact that their members came from the wealthiest sections of Roman society meant that they were most likely well-armoured, wearing some form of *lorica hamata* or comparable Hellenistic cuirasses. They carried either small circular ox-hide or Greek *clipeus*-type shields that would evolve into the *parma equestris*, and would have carried swords (almost certainly of the *gladius Hispaniensis* type) and spears. (Image courtesy of Kim Hawkins)

been training for war and command from the age of 17, and as most of them likely had political ambitions they would have to serve through at least ten campaigns before they would be eligible for election to public office, making the majority of them rather experienced as well (Daly 2002: 76). The 300 horsemen of a legion would be complemented by 600 from that legion's *ala*, presumably organized and led in a similar fashion to that of the Romans, with the riders most likely drawn from the ranks of the allied region's aristocrats and the well-to-do.

Carthaginian

The Numidians formed one of the Carthaginian army's most effective cavalry forces. Drawn from two North African Berber kingdoms, the Masaesyli (Masinissa's people) and the Massyli, Numidian horsemen were born to a life on horseback, learning to ride from a young age without saddles or conventional bridles (control of the horse being managed by the use of a plaited rope around the animal's neck); their mounts were small, rather scrawny ponies that seemed puny in comparison to the bigger and better-fed Roman mounts, but which proved to be hardy, nimble and able to endure much punishment. The Numidians were most likely organized in small troops of 30–40 horsemen as opposed to the larger homogenous tribal cavalry of the Gauls or Celtiberians (Daly 2002: 92), and wore no armour, carrying only a light shield and a handful of javelins. Their primary tactic was to dash in close to their enemy, discharge a volley of spears and ride away before their enemies could close and force a hand-to-hand engagement, something that may have led to some of the dismissive views of them as cowardly and prone to excessive flight when beaten.

Hannibal also had around 2,000 Iberian cavalry with him during his descent into Italia, most likely armed and armoured in the Hellenistic pattern (cuirass or mail coat, helmet, shield and spear), but his Gaulish allies brought enough horsemen to more than match the numbers of his Numidians and Iberians combined, 4,000 of them remaining by the time of Cannae. Drawn from the wealthiest and most important elements of Gaulish tribal societies, the horsemen were a social and military elite; they most likely operated in self-contained war bands of varying size, with each group following a particular noble or chieftain and his retinue. They were armed with heavy spears for thrusting rather than throwing, and the long cutting swords common to Celtic peoples; protection came in the form of helmets, shields and a much higher proportion of mail coats than would likely be found among the Celtic foot soldiers. Tactics would be rather simple, not dissimilar to the practice among Gaulish foot troops, with particular attention paid to displays of martial vigour and perhaps horsemanship as well.

The reverse of a Carthaginian gold *stater* (a coin originating from Greece, originally silver, the gold versions being worth 20–28 *drachmae*) depicting a wild horse, 4th century BC. The Carthaginian cavalry was, like the infantry, a heterogeneous affair consisting of North African tribal contingents (the most famous being the Numidians), as well as bodies of Iberians and Gauls, the latter two being formed of the most prestigious and wealthy warriors and their attendants, probably in loose groups of 100–200 horsemen. As with the infantry, Carthaginian cavalry units were organized according to their national and tribal groupings, each section fighting in their own traditional manner, quite unlike the practised homogeneity that could be found among the ranks of the Roman horse and their *alae*. (DEA/G. DAGLI ORTI/ De Agostini/Getty Images)

Numidian cavalry (at right) depicted in Scene LXIV on Trajan's Column, early 2nd century AD. During the Second Punic War, the Numidians were considered the best cavalry in North Africa. They were natural horsemen and rode without the aid of saddle, bit or bridle, controlling their mounts with a simple rope around the animal's neck, a stick and vocal commands. They seem to have worn little or no armour, relying instead on their speed and agility to avoid trouble, while their main weapon was the javelin or light spear. (Conrad Cichorius/Wikimedia/Public Domain)

An image of Mars (left) and a scene featuring two legionaries and an *eques* (right) from the Altar of Domitius Ahenobarbus (*c.*122–115 BC). For the Roman soldier, public recognition of his bravery was a crucial motivating factor in his decision to fight – and fight well. Military glory was raw meat to ambitious Romans of every class. It was not so difficult to see glory won on the field of battle as an expression of divine favour, which in turn encouraged the sense that such glory was a virtue in and of itself. For a people as aggressive and militarily minded as the Romans, the knowledge that success in war brought wealth, fame and the admiration of all was seductive. (Jastrow/Wikimedia/CC BY-SA 4.0)

MORALE

Roman

The Roman people understood the value of warfare and actively sought the benefits that it could bring, namely wealth and prestige. The martial culture of the Roman state was not a discrete element of the body politic, but rather a fundamental aspect of being a Roman citizen. Such an attitude had been developing since the 4th century BC, and was fully formed for all to see by the time of the wars against Carthage, there being only a single instance prior to 151 BC where the citizenry exhibited even a slight pause before voting for war, and that case – against King Philip V of Macedon – was due to the fact that it came fast on the heels of the end of the Second Punic War, a time when even the Romans may have sought some respite from constant conflict (Harris 2016: 39).

Service in the city's legions was commonplace among the citizenry, with a young man of the levy knowing that his grandfathers, father and older brothers had trodden the same path before him, the stories of their service augmented with battle trophies or keepsakes, not to mention the arms and armour that would have been a feature of every citizen's household, physical representations of the duty that was owed and the prosperity it could bring. When he entered the legion a Roman would find himself in an environment where acts of bravery could be recognized by his fellow legionaries and officers, resulting in the awarding of battle decorations that would secure his honour in both civilian and military life; a good indication of the esteem in which such awards were held is demonstrated by the fact that at religious processions the only decorations a man was allowed to wear were those that he had won by virtue of his own bravery on the battlefield (McDonnell 2006: 184–85).

The reality of life as a Roman soldier was certainly brutal, but the men who fought and killed on such a grand scale in Rome's wars did so from within a system – the legion – that was well-organized and gave a sense of security and belonging. Discipline was harsh and public, encouraging not just obedience but a broad sense of intolerance towards cowardice or the attitudes that might encourage it. The older men, the centurions and senior officers would all serve as examples of bravery in the face of the enemy, stiffening the resolve of newer, younger legionaries. The practice of maniples camping, marching, training and fighting together encouraged cohesion and a sense of purpose. The smallest unit – the *contubernium* – was a group of eight tent-mates who would quickly come to know and understand one another, such familiarity being invaluable when it came to standing shoulder to shoulder in order to receive a Gaulish charge. It is possible that several of the legions that fought at Cannae suffered from being freshly raised, put into the field before they had a chance to develop the strong bonds of trust that came from training and experience.

For the allies of Rome the need to send considerable levies of men on a regular basis must have been onerous, but it is not unreasonable to assume that they enjoyed similar benefits to their Roman associates when victories were won. There must also have been a deeper sense of the value in continued relationships with Rome, otherwise Hannibal's attempts to drag the Italian and Latin states out from under the great city's shadow would have been more successful. Certainly such ties must have been strained during the worst of the Carthaginian depredations of 218–216 BC, and yet the system of patronage and support that Rome had built withstood such serious threats remarkably well.

Carthaginian

Morale is of particular importance in armies like those fielded by Carthage, especially when they were of an expeditionary nature, sometimes spending years in a hostile land far from home. That basic fact was further complicated by the varied mix of contingents that went to make up such an army, men who came from different places, with different cultures and who spoke different languages, and who also most likely had very different reasons for deciding to fight in the first place.

For some of the North African contingents closest to the Carthaginian state there may have been some sense of patriotic obligation, but in most cases the larger narratives – love of Carthage or resentment of Rome – probably played a secondary role to more immediate concerns (though it is reasonable to assume that for several of the Gaulish tribes who flocked to Hannibal's banner as he made his way down from the Alps, an active dislike of their violent neighbours to the south did his recruiting efforts no harm). Hannibal built his army through a network of alliances that all provided some benefit (or at least the prospect of it) to those who threw in their lot with him rather than the Romans or anyone else; strong friends were always useful to local chieftains, and the prospects for booty that a commander could offer, particularly a successful one like Hannibal, were highly attractive.

Finally, the personal merits of the man whom they were choosing to serve must have had a considerable impact on the decision to join such an army, and especially to stay with it when the shadows began to close in. Hannibal delivered victory after victory to those that followed him (at least in the early years), but even through the campaigns of 219–216 BC there were reverses, hardship and the very real possibility of a violent end many hundreds of kilometres from home. Hannibal's charisma, generalship and personal qualities bound the leaders and chieftains of the many different contingents of his army to him, and through them came the loyalty of the men they led in their turn.

LEADERSHIP AND COMMAND

It was difficult for a commander to communicate effectively with his army once battle was joined, with messages carried by dispatch-riders being the most likely method employed. Pre-arranged signals could also play a role (it is likely that something of the sort was used at Trasimene to trigger Hannibal's ambush), while units engaged in battle would take their direction from the example set by their immediate leaders, the movement of their unit's standards, shouted orders, and signals sent out by musicians. For example, the Romans used *cornicenes* (horn-players), one of whom would be attached to each century under the command of the centurion, to issue tactical and movement orders that could be heard over the din of battle.

Roman

By the time of the Punic Wars the men who led Rome were entirely wedded to a system of dynamic expansion when the opportunity offered, with a senatorial class that was in thrall to the example of personal glory and honour won through martial endeavour, a position that in turn supported their own domestic financial and political interests (Harris 2016: 38–39). It was important for all Roman soldiers, especially ambitious commanders desirous of high office, to be seen performing acts of bravery or martial skill in the face of the enemy, such demonstrations earning them not just personal glory but also likely professional advancement.

The command of an army (usually two legions and two *alae*) would fall to one of the city's two consuls; when individual armies combined (such as at Cannae) the two consuls would command on alternate days – a system with several glaringly obvious flaws. Command of each individual legion fell to tribunes, whereas an *ala* was administered by a *praefectus* (prefect) of the allies. Each legion had six tribunes elected every year who also shared leadership duties, two tribunes running the legion together for two months at a time on a six-month rotation, while their compatriots would be at the disposal of the legion's consul, undertaking a variety of staff-related activities while they awaited their turn in command. At the lower level centurions took responsibility for maniples (decurions for cavalry *turmae*), supported by *optiones*, one *optio* per century (Daly 2002: 58–59).

Roman commanders projected authority and confidence by their presence on the field, so it was important that they could be seen easily. To that end their appearance was designed to set them apart from the rank and file, with senior officers wearing a distinctive cloak called a *paludamentum* as a sign of their office, and though shades of red, purple or white were the most common for such a garment, there does not seem to have been a set colour. It is likely that armour, cloaks, adornments and crests were common features among the legions' senior officers and centurions, as they too relied on being visible to their men so that they could ensure that their tactical orders were seen, as well as to stiffen morale (Gilliver 2007: 12–13). The distinctive transverse crest seems to have been closely associated with centurions, certainly in the Imperial period (27 BC onwards), though there is evidence for its use in the mid-Republican period and perhaps earlier as well.

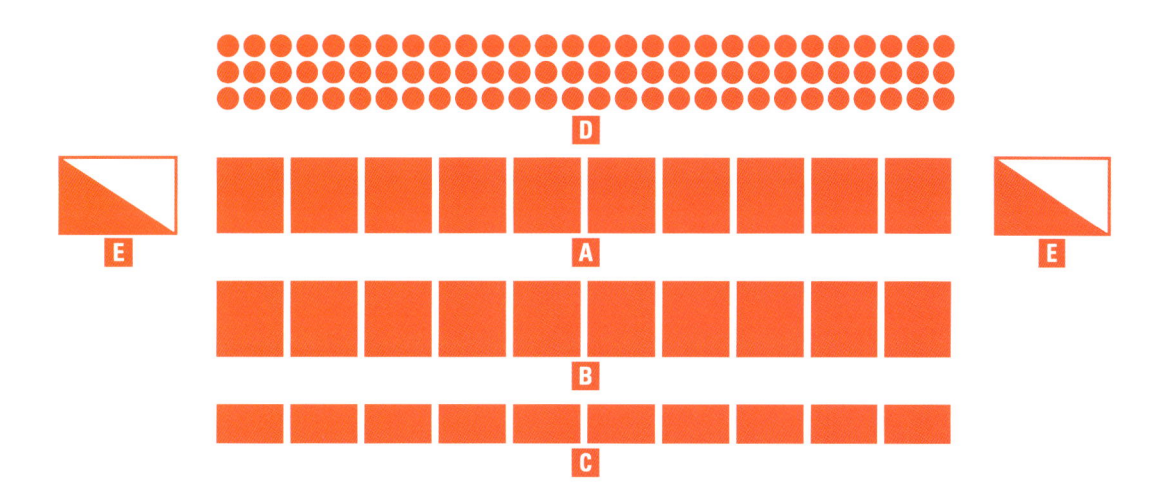

On the battlefield the role of a commander was to decide upon his objectives, establish the disposition of his troops, and make his wishes known to his subordinates. Once battle was joined a commander was limited in what he would be able to see, and changes he could make. To overcome these limitations of personal command, success in battle relied on detailed planning as well as the delegation of specific tasks or sections of the army to trusted officers (Sabin 1996: 68–69), and though such dispositions could not always react to the kinetic realities of a battle, they provided a framework within which an army's commanders understood their leader's overall objective, and the roles they were expected to play in securing that outcome.

Carthaginian

Hannibal was, along with Scipio, among the pre-eminent commanders of his age. He exemplified the role of battlefield generalship in his understanding of the capabilities, as well as the limitations, of his troops, his appreciation of his enemy's goals and behaviour, and his tactical sense when it came to choosing and using terrain to his advantage. In the heat of battle Hannibal, much like the other Carthaginian generals and their Roman opponents, would have been restricted in what he could do once battle was joined, his direct impact being limited to those men who could see him or receive his orders more or less directly (Sabin 1996: 68).

A Roman legion's infantry elements were organized into three main lines (the *triplex acies*), the first being the *hastati* (**A**); the *principes* (**B**) made up the second line, and the *triarii* (**C**) made up the third and final line. The youngest, and probably poorest men, made up the *velites* (**D**), the legion's light infantry who would deploy as a skirmish line to screen the main body of the legion from the enemy's light troops. The cavalry element, the *equites* (**E**), would operate on the army's wings. Each of the three main lines of infantry was divided into ten maniples of 120 men each (60 for the *triarii*), allowing the relatively shallow Roman lines much flexibility both in manoeuvring on the battlefield and in sustaining the pressure on an enemy line when engaged in combat. Each legion had an associated allied contingent, an *ala*, that presumably matched it in terms of composition and organization (though with double the number of cavalry), allowing Roman and allied units to manoeuvre and fight together coherently.

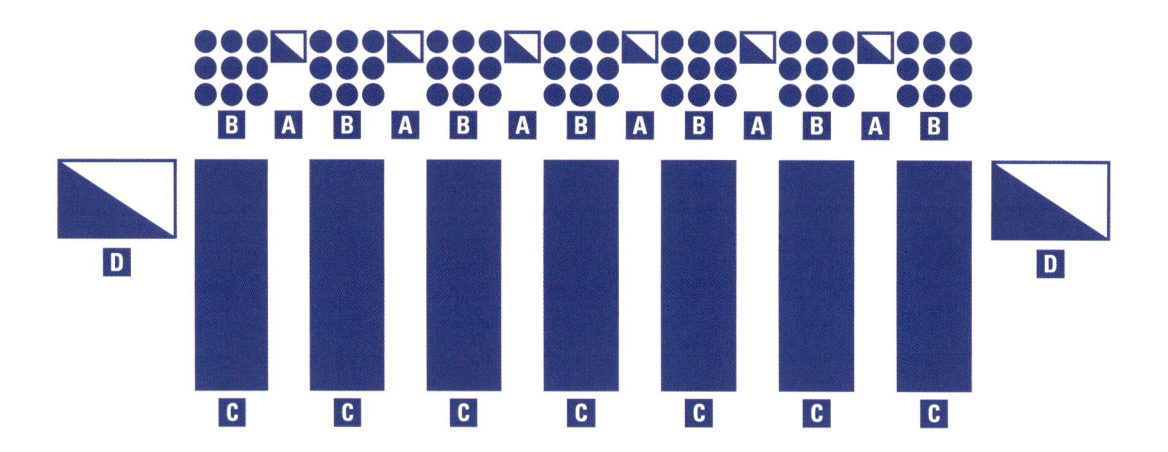

If they were available the front of a Carthaginian army would be screened by a line of elephants (**A**) positioned around 30m from one another, the gaps between them filled with light infantry (**B**) who were usually some combination of Iberian *caetrati*, Balearian slingers and Celts (drawn from Celto-Iberian or Gaulish tribes). The main line of infantry (**C**) would be composed of Iberian *scutarii*, Gauls and Libyo-Phoenician spear- or pike-armed heavy troops, divided by nationality (for example the line might be made up of blocks of Iberians alternating with Gauls and both ends anchored by the Libyo-Phoenicians, as at Cannae). Such dispositions were necessary where there was no consistency between the training or tactics of each national contingent. The cavalry (**D**), a mix of Gaulish, Iberian and Numidian units, would be positioned on the army's wings. The significant victories enjoyed by Hannibal in the early stages of the war were not so much a result of how his army was composed but rather a consequence of how he utilized it on a grand tactical scale, with detailed planning and the wise use of ground being critical factors in the successes he enjoyed.

Much of the most important work, therefore, was done before battle was ever joined; assembling forces, gaining allies, drilling the army for the task at hand, planning campaigns that maximized one's advantages while thwarting those of the enemy, all of which would nurture the development of a strong strategic position that would give one the best possible chance of victory on the day of battle (Sabin 1996: 77). In the Carthaginian case this was particularly important as the armies were a disparate collection of forces that had their own styles of fighting, their own methods of leadership, and their own reasons for taking to the field of battle on any given day. The great strength of Hannibal (and by extension the other Carthaginian commanders) was in his understanding that it was better to allow such contingents to retain their distinctiveness rather than trying to enforce a uniform standard of arms and tactics upon them. Instead, the Carthaginian model would use each contingent to its best advantage within an overarching tactical approach, something that absolutely required a very high degree of intelligent leadership if it was to work; obviously it was necessary for such a general to be intimately familiar with every contingent in his army, but he also had to command the trust and respect of the leaders of those contingents, making his role as much a political as a military one. Hannibal's performance at Lake Trasimene is a good example of both excellent planning and the ability to make the most of different troop types with varying tactical styles on the same battlefield at the same time.

Other major Carthaginian leaders included Hannibal's brothers, Hasdrubal and Mago, while Hasdrubal Gisco was one of the most important commanders outside the Barcid family. The Carthaginians were also fortunate in having not just very good cavalry, but excellent men to lead them, including Maharbal, Hannibal's trusted lieutenant, and the North African Masinissa, who made a name for himself in the battles in Iberia before he went over to the Romans in 206 BC. It is likely that the distinct ethnic groupings that made up the Carthaginian army would have been led by their own lords and chieftains, with higher command (over heterogeneous groups of infantry and cavalry, special detachments, or large tactical units such as the wings of an army) being exercised by Hannibal's proven lieutenants.

Lake Trasimene

June 217 BC

BACKGROUND TO BATTLE

As the winter of 218/217 BC drew in its horns, Hannibal, victor of Ticinus and the Trebia a few short months beforehand, had a decision to make. The trials he and his army had endured on their march from Iberia had been rewarded with new Gaulish allies and the destruction of a Roman army, but there was much still to do before his enemy of choice would lie broken before him. His strategy was designed to prise Rome's allies throughout Italia from its grip, denuding Rome of the manpower, money and strength that it would need to have any chance of defeating him. He aimed to accomplish this through a mixture of battlefield victories that undermined Rome's military capabilities, as well as by an ongoing provocative political campaign to try to cajole Rome's allies from its side.

Hannibal's overthrow of the consular legions sent against him at the Trebia had spurred a naturally aggressive Roman reaction, with two new armies sent out to thwart any attempts he might make to strike towards central Italia – the first, led by Gaius Flaminius Nepos, marched to Arretium (Arezzo), the second, under Gnaeus Servilius Geminus, was further to the east on the other side of the Apennines, taking up position at Ariminum (Rimini), both well-established by the beginning of spring 217 BC. Flaminius could block Hannibal if he tried to move south into Etruria (Tuscany), while Servilius could contain any move he might make down the eastern flank of the Apennines towards the Adriatic coast.

Hannibal was well aware that he could not rest on his newly won laurels. To prosecute his war effectively he had to move deeper into Italia and force the issue, making the Romans dance to his tune. His most obvious options were to move on Ariminum before hooking west into the Metaurus valley

An Iberian buckle and plate, dated to around the 5th century BC. The broad leather belts with their large buckles and plates are one of the most distinctive identifying features of Iberian culture, and seem to have been widely worn by light infantry, and perhaps also by heavy infantry (as always when dealing with such ancient artefacts, supposition takes over where supporting evidence is scant). (Metropolitan Museum of Art, www.metmuseum.org)

which would lead him out into the Tiber valley. The problem with such a plan was the length of time it would take, time that would most likely allow the two consuls opposing him to bring their armies together and face him with numerical parity. The alternative, which Hannibal chose, was to cross the Apennines at a more northerly latitude and then strike south, a more provocative move as it was not only faster but it positioned him to become a direct threat to Rome. The journey, carried out in harsh spring weather, proved gruelling for Hannibal as well as his army, costing him an eye due to an untreated infection, but soon enough he and his men were through the worst, taking a few days to recuperate at Faesulae (Fiesole). If there was a time for Flaminius to have attacked Hannibal with some chance of success, this was probably it, with his army (and Hannibal himself) worn and tired from a gruelling trek through icy mountain passes and chilling swamps, but there is no record of Flaminius even realizing that his enemy was barely 80km away – a reconnaissance failing that, in light of what was to follow, does not seem so strange (Lancel 1999: 92).

In short order Hannibal's army had recovered its vigour and set off down into Etruria, burning and despoiling all that lay in its path. By all accounts Hannibal's behaviour was a calculated act of aggression designed to provoke a reaction from Flaminius, an unusual, impetuous man. The Roman's actions throughout the Trasimene campaign earned him a great deal of opprobrium from the Greek and Latin historians who recorded his endeavours in later ages, some of it no doubt as a result of his calamitous failure, but also perhaps in part because he did not fit the mould of a great patrician. His family had no significant standing in Rome, and his reputation was as something of a demagogue, rousing the people to help him get what he wanted in exchange for populist measures such as land distribution and building programmes, but in the febrile world of Roman politics it is extremely difficult to come to a fair judgement about such behaviour, every act being interpreted any number of ways (many of them malicious) by others for their own particular ends. What does seem certain is that Flaminius lacked the military experience of his fellow consul Servilius, and was either impetuous, arrogant or both; his actions leading up to the battle at Trasimene bear out such a view. In the event Hannibal's rampage through the countryside was the goad that set Flaminius after him.

There were several advantages for Hannibal in getting the Roman army to break camp and try to hunt him down. First, though it might take Servilius some time to march to Flaminius' aid, he was presumably on his way, so any strategy that drew the two forces further apart was obviously beneficial. Second, the Carthaginians did not operate from fixed depots and supply lines, preferring instead to live off the land as they went. The advantages of such a method of feeding one's force were the flexibility of movement it usually afforded, as well as no need to garrison supply routes or to worry about the enemy cutting them; the main disadvantage was the need to keep moving – it did not take long for an army of 50,000 men together with thousands of horses and pack animals to strip an area bare. Third, by drawing Flaminius out Hannibal could retain the strategic initiative, giving him more and better opportunities to exploit than if he were to let Flaminius come to him (Goldsworthy 2006: 185).

In the event Flaminius had little luck in pinning his enemy down. Hannibal moved southwards, apparently heading towards Rome; Flaminius closed the distance between them, the two forces eventually being less than a day's march from one another. Moving past the town of Cortona, the Carthaginians made a surprising turn to the east, taking then in the direction of Lake Trasimene, drawing the eager Romans in their wake, eventually slipping through the defile by Borghetto. Flaminius, following closely, opted to make camp near the entrance to the defile in anticipation of continuing his pursuit the following day.

A belt clasp made in the Iberian peninsula, 2nd century BC. This bronze and silver buckle is unusual in that both its top and bottom plaque are preserved, along with remains of the iron rivets used to attach it to a leather belt. Small figurines show warriors wearing similar clasps, suggesting this was designed for use by a soldier. It is typical of a type of buckle produced in the central plain region of the Iberian Peninsula, where silver is found in the Sierra Morena mountains. In design it is closely related to engraved examples of artwork found in Andalusia in the southwest of Spain. Opposing spirals were a popular motif in Celtic art and were often combined with concentric circles on buckles such as this one. The design was created by carving out a pattern on a bronze panel, and then hammering a thin sheet of silver into the indentations. (Metropolitan Museum of Art, www.metmuseum.org)

Lake Trasimene, 217 BC

MAP KEY

1 At 7am, Flaminius breaks camp, his legions forming column and marching towards what they assume to be a small Carthaginian rearguard set upon some high ground several kilometres to the east. The force passes through a narrow defile into a shallow basin of ground surrounded by high wooded hills on one side and Lake Trasimene on the other.

2 Hannibal springs his trap, attacking the column at its head, its rear, and all along its flank in a series of simultaneous assaults that take Flaminius and his men completely by surprise. The Romans are unable to deploy, with the general confusion compounded by the dense mist making it impossible for the commanders to know what is going on or to provide one another with mutual support.

3 The majority of the Roman line disintegrates; the rear of the column is driven into the lake and destroyed, while the main body of the force is broken down and overwhelmed.

4 Some 6,000 Romans from the head of the column drive through the ambush, unwittingly freeing themselves from the catastrophe developing behind them. They take refuge in a village a few kilometres distant, but are soon surrounded and forced to surrender.

Battlefield environment

The battle took place on the northern shore of Lake Trasimene in the early summer, the mist still lying heavy on the earth as the Romans marched obliviously along the low ground into their ambush. Polybius and Livy do not agree on the exact location of the battle, though most modern historians are certain that it took place on the northern shore in the basin known as Sanguineto; the hills remain more or less as they were (aside from construction), but the lake's shoreline has changed considerably over the centuries, with opinions varying as to the level of the waterline (and thus the actual size of the battle space) at the time of the ambush (Fields 2017). Along the Roman left flank (to the north) the ground rose up into a semicircle of heavily wooded hills split by winding valleys and pathways, while the right flank (to the south) ran down to patches of marshland and the shore of the lake. Directly ahead of the Roman line of march rose a high spur of land (the location of the modern town Tuoro sul Trasimeno), which Hannibal had manned with infantry, making it the left wing of his deployment. The battlefield that developed along the roadway would likely have been made up of scrubland, smallholdings and their accompanying fields, with no significant defensible structures or terrain.

An image of the northern shoreline of Lake Trasimene (Lago Trasimeno), showing the stretch of land that was the likely site of the destruction of Flaminius' army. The Romans entered from the left in column, unaware of Hannibal's men who were hidden among the wooded slopes in the foreground. The town on the right of the picture (Tuoro sul Trasimeno) is the probable location of Hannibal's left wing, the scene of the only successful Roman action on that day. (Tom Bennett/Wikimedia/CC BY-SA 3.0)

500 yd
500 m

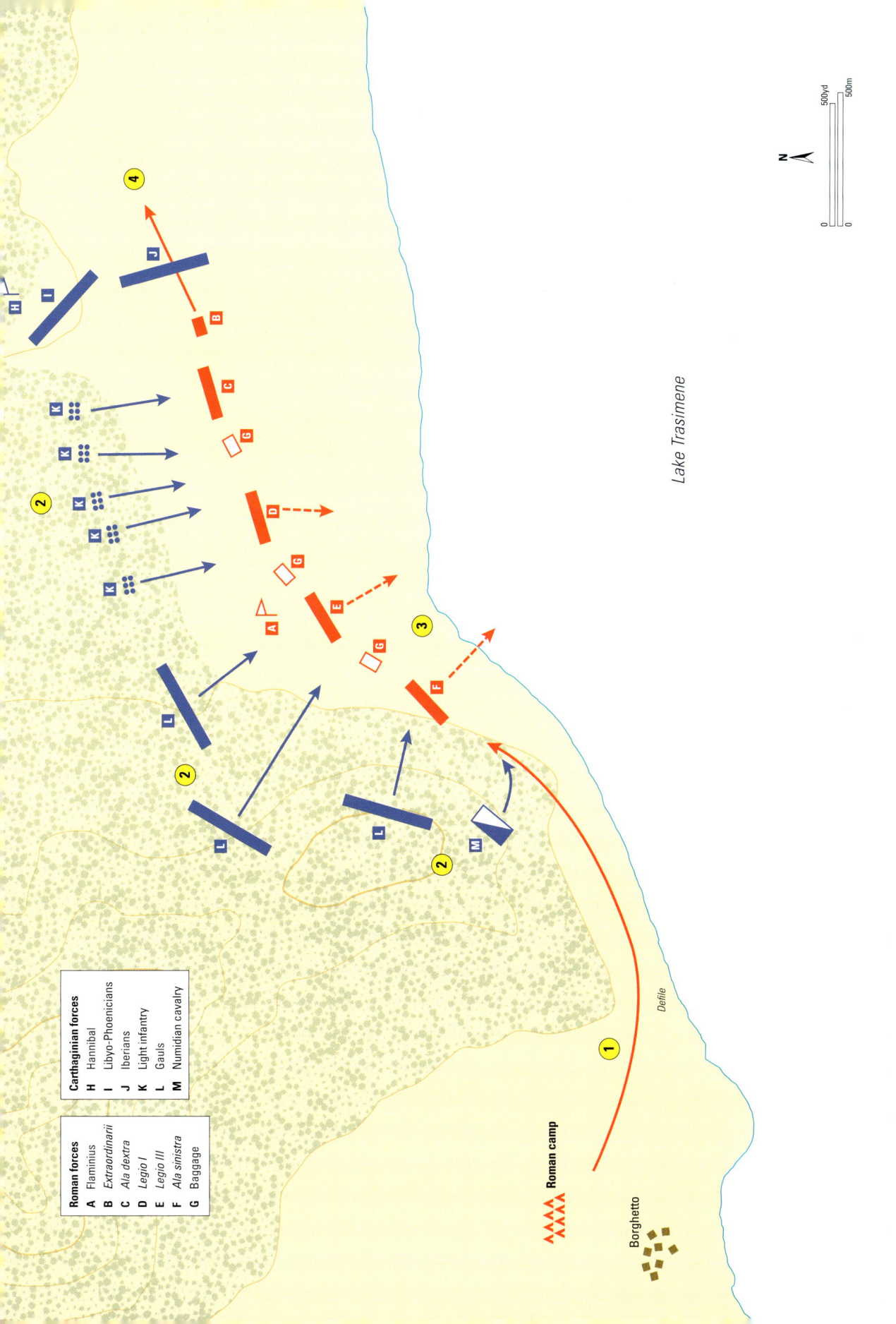

N

Lake Trasimene

Roman forces
A Flaminius
B Extraordinarii
C Ala dextra
D Legio I
E Legio III
F Ala sinistra
G Baggage

Carthaginian forces
H Hannibal
I Libyo-Phoenicians
J Iberians
K Light infantry
L Gauls
M Numidian cavalry

Defile

Roman camp

Borghetto

INTO COMBAT

The army that Flaminius fielded was of the standard consular type – two newly raised legions (*legio I* and *legio III*, made up from fresh levies of soldiers mixed with the remains of the consular armies that had survived the Trebia), with two *alae* as well – perhaps 25,000–30,000 men in all, of whom perhaps 1,800 were cavalry. The fact that the legions were fresh should not unduly prejudice our view of their performance; certainly there would be many new recruits, but plenty of the men who filled out the ranks of the *principes* and *triarii* would undoubtedly have served in previous campaigns, and the more callow members (found in the *hastati* and the *velites*) would still have had a serious amount of training before they even joined their centuries. The nominal strength of a fully manned legion was 4,500 legionaries, with 300 cavalry (5,400 men with 600 cavalry for an *ala*), though such numbers undoubtedly varied on campaign. There may well have been extra troops in the form of volunteers eager to accompany the army so as to be in on the victory, though they were probably Latin or Italian *socii* in origin rather than Roman.

The core of Hannibal's army were his Libyo-Phoenician heavy infantry, probably numbering around 8,000–12,000 men, supported by levies of Iberian *scutarii*; he also had considerable numbers of light troops, including more Iberian levies in the shape of javelin-wielding *caetrati*, as well as Balearian slingers. The various clans of the Gauls made up a significant number of his infantry and cavalry (somewhere around 20,000 foot and 5,000 horse – half his army – from tribes such as the Insubres and probably the Boii, among others), with his remaining horse comprised of Iberians and his contingent of Numidians, splendid North African light cavalry, all commanded by Maharbal. His total force numbered somewhere around 50,000 men, 10,000 of whom were mounted, offering a significant advantage, especially in cavalry, over Flaminius' army.

The Carthaginian actions in the days leading up to the battle are suggestive of an army looking either to outmanoeuvre its foe or to engage him in battle. Hannibal most likely wanted a fight, and quickly at that, bearing in mind the whereabouts of Servilius, which was an unknown factor and significant threat. With something like double Flaminius' strength Hannibal was well able to join battle with the Romans almost whenever he pleased, but he refused to do so; the Carthaginian was wary of unnecessary combat that would diminish his finite reserves of manpower, and a pitched battle, even with such good odds, would likely still prove to be a very costly affair. Attempting to tip the odds further in his favour was a natural and understandable way to proceed, especially if he could find a scenario to maximize the benefit of his own numbers while diminishing that of his opponent. It is possible that while he had Flaminius on the line Hannibal played for time, looking for an opportunity where he could force an engagement on the best possible terms, which he certainly seemed to find in the ambush site on the northern shores of Lake Trasimene. How long he might have known about the area, or when he decided that it would make the perfect trap in which to catch his hungry pursuer, will always be a matter of speculation. Irrespective of when he made the decision, the ground he chose was extremely promising for what he had in mind.

OPPOSITE
A drawing of a *gladius Hispaniensis* found on the island of Delos, Greece, dating from the 1st century BC. It retains its scabbard and the associated fittings. The *gladius* proved to be a highly effective weapon, excellently suited to legionary infantry tactics and intimidating for Rome's foes, as noted by Livy: 'those who, being always accustomed to fight with Greeks and Illyrians, had only seen wounds made with javelins and arrows, seldom even by lances, came to behold bodies dismembered by the Spanish sword, some with their arms lopped off, with the shoulder or the neck entirely cut through, heads severed from the trunk, and the bowels laid open, with other frightful exhibitions of wounds: they therefore perceived, with horror, against what weapons and what men they were to fight' (31.34.4). The *gladius* was an excellent all-round weapon, but it was most effective when used in conjunction with a *scutum*; for a legionary in formation, its ability to deliver short, deadly thrusts allowed the wielder to make the most of the protection his shield offered, limiting his exposure to his opponent's blows while still being able to drive home his own attack. (M.C. Bishop)

Livy describes the approach that the Romans would have to take to get at Hannibal, the ground being 'a place formed by nature for an ambuscade, where the Trasimenus comes nearest to the mountains of Cortona. A very narrow passage only intervenes, as though room enough just for that purpose had been left designedly; after that a somewhat wider plain opens itself, and then some hills rise up' (22.4.2). Hannibal had made his main camp on those hills, displaying ranks of his Libyo-Phoenicians and Iberians so that they could be seen with ease by any force approaching along the northern shore of the lake, a glittering fishhook for Flaminius. The head of the valley was stopped with Hannibal's heavy infantry; he took his light troops including the Balearic contingent together with his Gaulish allies and concealed them in the wooded ravines and hills that overlooked the northern side of the road (the light troops on the eastern side, with the Gauls in the centre and on the left). To complete the deployment he placed Numidian and Iberian cavalry close to the mouth of the defile, well-concealed behind nearby hillocks, their role being to slam shut the door on any possible escape route for the Roman column, ensuring the legions could not go back the way they had come in.

Flaminius, sure that he was marching to catch an enemy doing its best to flee, does not seem to have considered any other option. He had been dogging Hannibal's footsteps for several days without ever coming close enough to force an engagement, but now it must have seemed to him that his enemy was just within his grasp. The Carthaginian campfires that burned through the night in open view would surely have given any sensible commander pause, especially considering the occluded nature of the terrain awaiting any army that might try to advance upon them, but for whatever reason Flaminius had made a fundamental mistake: he failed to understand that his army did not have the initiative, merely the appearance of it.

The next day (21 June according to Ovid) the Romans broke camp early, setting out at around 7am; the sun was up. The way ahead was dominated by a thick and persistent mist that obscured much from view, but which receded on the upper slopes of a series of hills a little over 3km due east. There Flaminius could see unmistakable ranks of Carthaginian soldiers, a rearguard, he must have assumed, set upon the high ground to further delay his pursuit of Hannibal's main force. Though neither Polybius nor Livy give a description of the Roman column of march at Trasimene, elsewhere Polybius does give an example of how such a column should be disposed: first would come the *extraordinarii* (the best troops drawn from the *alae*), followed by the *ala dextra* (the allied legion of the right wing) and its baggage, then *legio I* and its baggage, then *legio III* and its baggage, then the baggage of the *ala sinistra* (the allied legion of the left wing) which itself comes last, forming the rearguard. Cavalry would ride either at the rear of their respective units or with the baggage animals to help keep them together and protected (Fields 2017: 73).

Marching on the track that ran close to the shore of Lake Trasimene, Flaminius and his army filtered through the narrow defile at the western end of the road and into the broader fields that lay beyond; the Carthaginians stood out clear in the near distance, their ranks waiting on the high clear crest of the hills that lay directly in the Roman line of march. As the long column of the army snaked its way between the rough wooded hills on one side and the broad expanse of the lake on the other, fully entering the shallow basin of

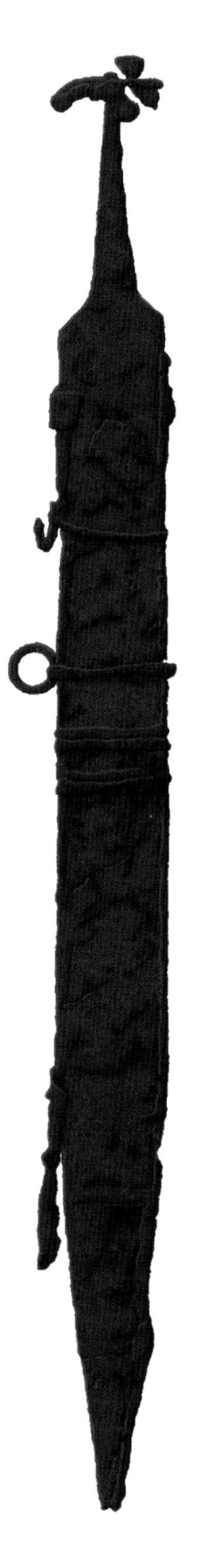

Gaius Flaminius Nepos

Flaminius does not emerge well from the accounts of Livy and Polybius, and there seems little doubt that his tactical and strategic leadership was a significant factor in the disaster at Trasimene, but like other men of his position such military responsibilities were indivisible from his civic duty. He was a *novus homo* – a 'new man', the first of his family to rise to the Senate – who enjoyed a controversial but apparently popular and certainly successful political life, being elected consul twice. Though portrayed as a demagogue who rode to his political victories on the backs of the plebs, it is highly unlikely that he could have risen so far and so fast without patronage from some of the more powerful factions in Roman high society. Though his martial inexperience is cited as a reason for his failure against Hannibal, he had led an army over the Po River and defeated the Gaulish Insubres in battle in 223 BC, and bearing in mind the Roman attitude to personal valour and military experience it does not seem likely that he would have been successful in his political endeavours if he was regarded by his contemporaries as excessively rash or incompetent in such a role. In the wake of the obloquy heaped on him by Livy, Polybius and others for reasons that likely extend far beyond his last great military failing, it is difficult to separate the man from the caricature.

ground that preceded the heights on which their brazen foe waited, Hannibal watched. The moment that the leading elements of the *extraordinarii* came into contact with his Libyo-Phoenician and Iberian veterans, he gave the order to attack, determined to deliver 'an assault upon the enemy at every point at once' (Polybius 3.84).

All along the length of the Roman column's left flank Gauls, Iberians and Balearians came boiling out of the dense banks of mist and hurled themselves on their stunned enemy; the head of the column found itself under attack as well, with the rear echelon set upon by waves of Carthaginian horsemen who seemed to have appeared from nowhere. The shock of the attack was amplified by the dense mist that made it impossible for the centurions and tribunes to have any clear idea of what was happening, or where, leaving them unable to organize any coherent defence or to support those parts of the column that were under the most serious attack. The individual units within the column had no time to organize even a rudimentary deployment, denying the Romans one of their most significant tactical advantages and allowing the wild individualistic character of Gaulish warfare to show itself to best effect. The ferocity of the attack was compounded by the showers of javelins and slingshot that must have rained down on the densely packed groups of legionaries, targets that were impossible to miss, as well as by the depredations of the Numidian and Iberian horseman who were tearing at the column's hindquarters.

The situation was particularly dismal near the defile, where the nimble Carthaginian horsemen had blocked any retreat. Unable to advance or fall back and with no space to execute any sort of deployment, all sense of cohesion disintegrated, with many of the legionaries fleeing into the deceptively safe waters of the lake:

> some in their frantic terror endeavoured to swim with their armour on, and presently sank and were drowned; while the greater number, wading as far as they could into the lake, remained there with their heads above water; and when the cavalry rode in after them, and certain death stared them in the face, they raised their hands and begged for quarter, offering to surrender, and using every

Maharbal

Hannibal's most important cavalry commander in the early years of the Second Punic War, Maharbal made important contributions to Carthaginian success on the battlefield, having been with the army at least since the siege at Saguntum in 219–218 BC. The son of Himilco (possibly a descendant of the Magonid dynasty, an important Carthaginian family whose great days were long behind them), his date of birth is unknown. At Trasimene his cavalry, fresh from the field of battle, hunted down and captured the Romans who had escaped the worst of that day's bloodshed, a feat he followed up in even more spectacular fashion shortly afterwards. Gnaeus Servilius Geminus' army at Ariminum had dispatched Gaius Centenius with a force of 4,000 horse in support of Flaminius, unaware of the disaster that had befallen the Roman commander and his men. Upon hearing of this new force, Hannibal sent Maharbal with a combined force of cavalry and light infantry to intercept it, which he did in what was almost a miniature repeat of Trasimene, killing half the Romans in the initial encounter and pursuing the rest before capturing them the next day. He may well have been at Cannae (Livy and Appian think so, but Polybius does not mention him). The last mention of Maharbal is at the siege of Casilinum at the end of 216 BC, after which nothing more is known of him.

imaginary appeal for mercy; but were finally despatched by the enemy, or, in some cases, begged the favour of the fatal blow from their friends, or inflicted it on themselves. (Polybius 3.84)

Of the Roman and allied horsemen no mention is made in Livy or Polybius, even though several thousand of them must have been trapped in the ambush with the rest of the army. It is probable that, if they were split up among the various sections of the column as was the common practice, they were quickly hemmed-in just as the infantry were, with even less room to manoeuvre or to organize themselves, failing to fight back or take the chance to break out.

Flaminius was somewhere near the centre of the column when the hammer fell, most likely riding with *legio III*, no doubt doing his best to salvage something from the nightmare that was rapidly developing around him. Livy gives a dramatic (if possibly romanticized) account of his fate. The consul was at the heart of the fiercest fighting, personally leading bands of the strongest legionaries into the most desperate parts of the fray to keep his hard-pressed men from cracking, exhorting them to stand fast and fight because only martial valour could save them, not wails and prayers to the gods, but despite his best efforts the roiling confusion of the battle drowned out all his pleas and attempts to assert command. His own men may have had difficulty heeding him, but his distinctive armour signalled his status to friend and foe alike, and he soon became the focus of repeated severe attacks, only kept at bay by the exertions of some of his veteran soldiers. Into this maelstrom came an Insubrian horseman named Ducarius who recognized Flaminius as the man responsible for much suffering among his people during a campaign he had conducted through the tribal lands six years previously. Setting his heels to his horse's flanks, Ducarius charged through a throng of *triarii*, first killing Flaminius' armour-bearer before coming down on the consul himself, running him through with a spear and thus ending his part in the battle. One account had Ducarius hacking off Flaminius' head and bearing it aloft in triumph, much to the dismay of those who saw it. For Polybius the end was rather more prosaic, with Flaminius 'in a state of the utmost distress and despair' (3.84), set upon and cut down by a band of Gauls. Hannibal searched for the consul's

A bronze Montefortino-type helmet with cheek-guards, Etruscan, late 4th century BC. Probably inspired by Celtic prototypes, Montefortino-type helmets were especially popular in Etruria from the 4th to the 2nd centuries BC. The commanders of armies in the classical period were well aware that appearance mattered. The Greek writer Onasander, discussing the requirements of generalship in the 1st century AD, noted that 'The general should make it a point to draw up his line of battle resplendent in armour – an easy matter, requiring only a command to sharpen swords and to clean helmets and breast-plates. For the advancing companies appear more dangerous by the gleam of weapons, and the terrible sight brings fear and confusion to the hearts of the enemy' (28). Though Roman arms and armour of the mid-Republican era were likely much more varied than those of the late Republican or early Imperial periods, there was enough consistency for a force to present a coherent, threatening face to an opponent, especially if that force were as well-drilled and -disciplined as the Roman legions were. (Metropolitan Museum of Art, www.metmuseum.org)

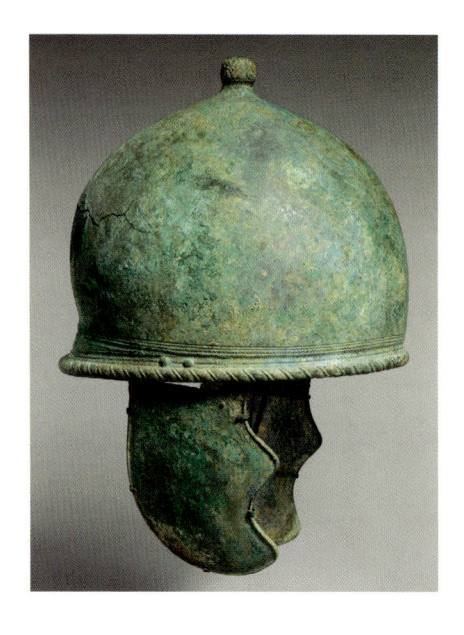

body after the battle, intent on giving it a proper burial, but stripped and no doubt mutilated as Flaminius then was, it was impossible to pick him out from the thousands of bodies that lay beside him.

The loss of their leader would certainly have had a debilitating effect on the legionaries who witnessed his demise, but in such a ferocious and confused fight the death of Flaminius almost certainly went unnoticed by all but those nearest to him. Even had he survived Ducarius' attack there would have been little he could have done to save his army from its fast-arriving fate. The careful order of the *triplex acies* was nowhere to be found as the cohesion of the column distorted and began to splinter under the fury of the Gaulish warriors and their long, slashing swords; individual legionaries could not even make out their own standards, let along their place in the line, with many no doubt also still burdened by their marching packs. The constant clamour of fighting mingled with war cries, screams and the sounds of weapons hammering down on heads, arms and bodies, all in one great disorganized mass, likely led to not just fear but terror in men who drew strength from knowing their place, from sleeping and drilling and fighting in the same way with the same set of men from their *contubernium*, shoulder to shoulder.

Attempts at escape were confounded because it was impossible to know which way to go, with apparent openings suddenly closed off by a sudden burst of fighting, or blocked by groups of men coming back who had already tried and failed to get away. Livy observed that

> After charges had been attempted unsuccessfully in every direction, and on their flanks the mountains and the lake, on the front and rear the lines of the enemy enclosed them, when it was evident that there was no hope of safety but in the right hand and the sword; then each man became to himself a leader, and encourager to action. (22.5.6–7)

Such individual endeavour was hardly unknown in Roman warfare, which paid particular attention to the glories that a man might win for himself on the field of battle, but Trasimene, in the space of a few short hours, was turning from a battle into a massacre in which personal prowess counted for very little. The remnants of cohesion that held the column together began to give way entirely, with men breaking away in wild panic and running blindly in any and every direction, tumbling over one another in their desperation to get clear of the killing field, but there was nowhere to go. Now it was just a matter of time.

A Montefortino-type helmet (Etruscan, 4th–3rd centuries BC) that would have been a common sight in the mid-Republican legion. The helmet has a hemispherical one-piece bowl of cast, hammered, chased, and engraved bronze, which is surmounted by an integral medial knob-shaped finial, and flanged at the rear into a sloped nape guard that slightly flares upward. It is robust, measuring up to 6.3mm in thickness at the rim, except at the rear, where it becomes thinner as the result of having been hammered into a nape guard. There are two bronze rivets with flush heads at each side of the helmet. These retain bronze washers and fragments of bronze hinges on the interior for attaching the cheek-pieces (which are now lost). There similarly is a bronze rivet with a flush head in the middle of the nape guard, which holds a hinged double bronze loop on the interior, for attaching chin straps. (Metropolitan Museum of Art, www.metmuseum.org)

A bronze helmet of Apulian-Corinthian type, mid-4th–mid-3rd century BC. Such helmets usually sported crests, with many examples having fittings to accept feathers on either side of the dome as well. The eyeholes and nose-guard on Apulian-Corinthian helmets were purely decorative, as the fashion was to wear the helmet pushed back on the head. Though they certainly seemed to have been popular in southern Italy in the 4th century BC, it is difficult to say how common such helmets may have been in Roman armies by the time of the Second Punic War; the figure of Mars on the Altar of Domitius Ahenobarbus (*c.*122–115 BC; see page 24) might be wearing an Apulian-Corinthian helmet, but it is damaged and thus inconclusive. (Metropolitan Museum of Art, www.metmuseum.org)

The soldiers of the Roman vanguard, around 6,000 men in all made up of the *extraordinarii* and the *ala dextra*, managed to do what the rest of their column could not – they kept their heads and their cohesion despite the shocking and intense situation in which they found themselves. It was impossible for the vanguard to know what was happening along the rest of the line, though the sounds and screams they heard would certainly have given them a sense of how serious the situation was, and they were in no better a position than any other part of the army to understand the shape of the battle, or to see where their efforts would be best rewarded. In such a circumstance they attacked the enemy they could see, throwing themselves against the Libyo-Phoenician and Iberian heavy infantry that had closed off the road in front of them. They battled forward, pushing the Carthaginian line further and further back until the Romans broke through, emerging onto higher ground; it was only then, looking back at the heaving ruin of the army in the clearing mists below, that the true scale of what had happened dawned on them.

There was no help that could be offered in such a circumstance. The men of the vanguard gathered up their standards and made for a village some kilometres distant, but found themselves pursued through the night by Maharbal's cavalry as well as some detachments of light infantry. The Roman survivors gained the relative safety of the village, hungry and dispirited, only to find themselves soon surrounded by the pursuing Carthaginians. Maharbal knew that the upper hand was his, and no doubt the exhausted Romans did too; he offered them their lives and, for the non-Romans, their freedom as well if they would but lay down their arms, which they duly did. The defeated men were marched back to the main Carthaginian camp where they were added to the roster of captives, perhaps 15,000 in all. The Romans among them were kept as prisoners, while the Italians were released without ransom, Hannibal stating that he 'was not come to fight against Italians, but on behalf of Italians against Rome' (quoted in Polybius 3.85), an act in furtherance of his broader strategy of trying to drive a wedge between Rome and its network of supporting cities and states across Italia. (As an aside, the fact that the vanguard that broke out contained a mix of Romans and allied troops means that the probable layout of a Roman column listed earlier may be reasonable, the *extraordinarii* being drawn from allied units and given pride of place at the head of the march.)

The loss of the Roman army was total, with perhaps 15,000 killed and the rest falling into captivity. The Carthaginians had lost around 30 senior officers and 1,500 others (2,500 or more according to Livy), mostly Gauls; the heaps of Roman dead provided a windfall for many of the Carthaginian rank and file, the helmets, mail coats, swords and spears being stripped from their bodies in such numbers as to be able to re-equip whole units, including Hannibal's veteran Libyo-Phoenician heavy infantry phalanxes among others. The shock felt in Rome when news of the defeat came through was palpable in every section of the city, the scale of the catastrophe being too great to hide or belittle with weasel words. In such circumstances the practice was to select a *dictator* through a quick election – in this instance Quintus Fabius Maximus, soon to earn the sobriquet *cunctator* ('delayer') – to take matters in hand. Over the coming months Quintus Fabius would do exactly that, but in a manner that frustrated his fellow Romans more than it did Hannibal, with fateful consequences.

A Roman trilobate arrowhead, with a tang to fit into the shaft (as opposed to a socket). The main types of Roman arrowheads discovered through archaeological excavation have been mostly either trilobite or flat-bladed, and would likely have been shot from self-bows; *sagittarii* (archers) certainly would come to use the more powerful composite bow (both on foot and on horseback), but the chances are that this was after the Romans had engaged in significant military encounters with Eastern armies, from the late Republican period onwards. *Sagittarii* who served with the legions in the Punic Wars were to be found in the Latin *alae* rather than the Roman legions proper. (Image courtesy of Kim Hawkins)

Cannae

Summer 216 BC

BACKGROUND TO BATTLE

The calamity of Trasimene had focused Roman minds on the threat their state faced. Trebia had been a severe loss, but Trasimene was a humiliating disaster, an offence against the pride of Rome. The man who had stabilized Rome's fortunes in the wake of that shock, Quintus Fabius Maximus (insulted as 'the delayer'), had proved himself able to resist the poisonous temptation of engaging Hannibal in battle, but he had not managed to persuade his fellow citizens that such an approach was either effective or honourable. After he laid down his dictatorship a new, more combative strategy rapidly took shape under the new consuls elected in March, Lucius Aemilius Paullus and Gaius Terentius Varro, with the support of most of the citizenry.

Understanding the seriousness of the situation the Senate authorized the raising of four more legions with their associated *alae* – an unprecedented doubling of the consular armies. They would be added to the two existing consular armies led by Marcus Atilius Regulus (replaced with Marcus Minucius Rufus by the time of the battle) and Gnaeus Servilius Geminus, the previous year's consuls, who were currently shadowing Hannibal's army as it wintered in Geronium in Apulia (near the modern town of Castel Dragonara). The plan was simple enough: the new legions under Paullus and Varro would set out from Rome and join forces with the legions of Atilius and Servilius, whereupon they would take command of all four armies. Each consul would command the entire force on alternate days – a traditionally Roman method of splitting power, but a poor option for Paullus and Varro, two men with very different dispositions and widely varying ideas of how to best defeat Hannibal. Their brief from the Senate was clear: seek out an opportunity to force Hannibal into battle and then destroy him.

A bronze torso (Hellenistic or imperial, 2nd century BC–2nd century AD). Originally part of an equestrian statue, the figure wears a cuirass of *linothorax*-type design, this one with *pteruges* (strips of protective leather) at the shoulder. It is a good example of the sort of highly decorated distinctive personal armour that would be worn by senior officers of either Roman or Carthaginian armies during this period. (Metropolitan Museum of Art, www.metmuseum.org)

Hannibal's army left Geronium in early June 216 BC and made straight for Cannae, a ruined citadel 100km distant that served as a grain and food storage facility for the Roman army. His presence there would threaten the food production of the entire region, an act that could have serious consequences for the Roman state that relied upon the harvests from such areas (Healy 1994: 67). Hannibal's new tactic would allow his army to enjoy all the food it needed while provoking the Romans into sending another force against him – or to fail to do so, thus proving their impotence in the face of his depredations, which would be a potentially disastrous admission for Rome to make in front of its allies. Either way, Hannibal would get something he wanted. His army had come through the winter well, and was still extremely strong despite the fact that he had been campaigning in one form or another for over two and a half years. The addition of the Gauls had been critical as they now made up the best part of half his army (including a sizeable portion of his cavalry), but he could still rely on the various elements that made up the rest of his polyglot force, namely his Libyo-Phoenician heavy infantry, his Balearian slingers, the nimble Numidian horsemen on their wiry ponies, and the Iberians who performed as light infantry, heavy infantry and cavalry too.

News of Hannibal's move spurred Paullus and Varro, who quickly readied their new forces and left Rome, probably in late June, heading south-east to liaise with Atilius and Servilius, who had been gingerly shadowing the progress of Hannibal ever since he had vacated his winter quarters. Though the accounts of Livy and Polybius are clear that the consuls did not get along (and they each share a particularly dim view of Varro), both consuls must have considered the kind of strategy they would need to employ if they were to fulfil the wishes of the Roman people. The

A bronze cuirass, of Greek or Apulian manufacture, 4th century BC. The *musculata* ('muscled') style of cuirass had been fashionable with senior officers and the well-to-do since Archaic times, a popularity that continued down into both Roman and Carthaginian armies. The cuirass would be worn over a leather jerkin with *pteruges* at the shoulder and waist. (Metropolitan Museum of Art, www.metmuseum.org)

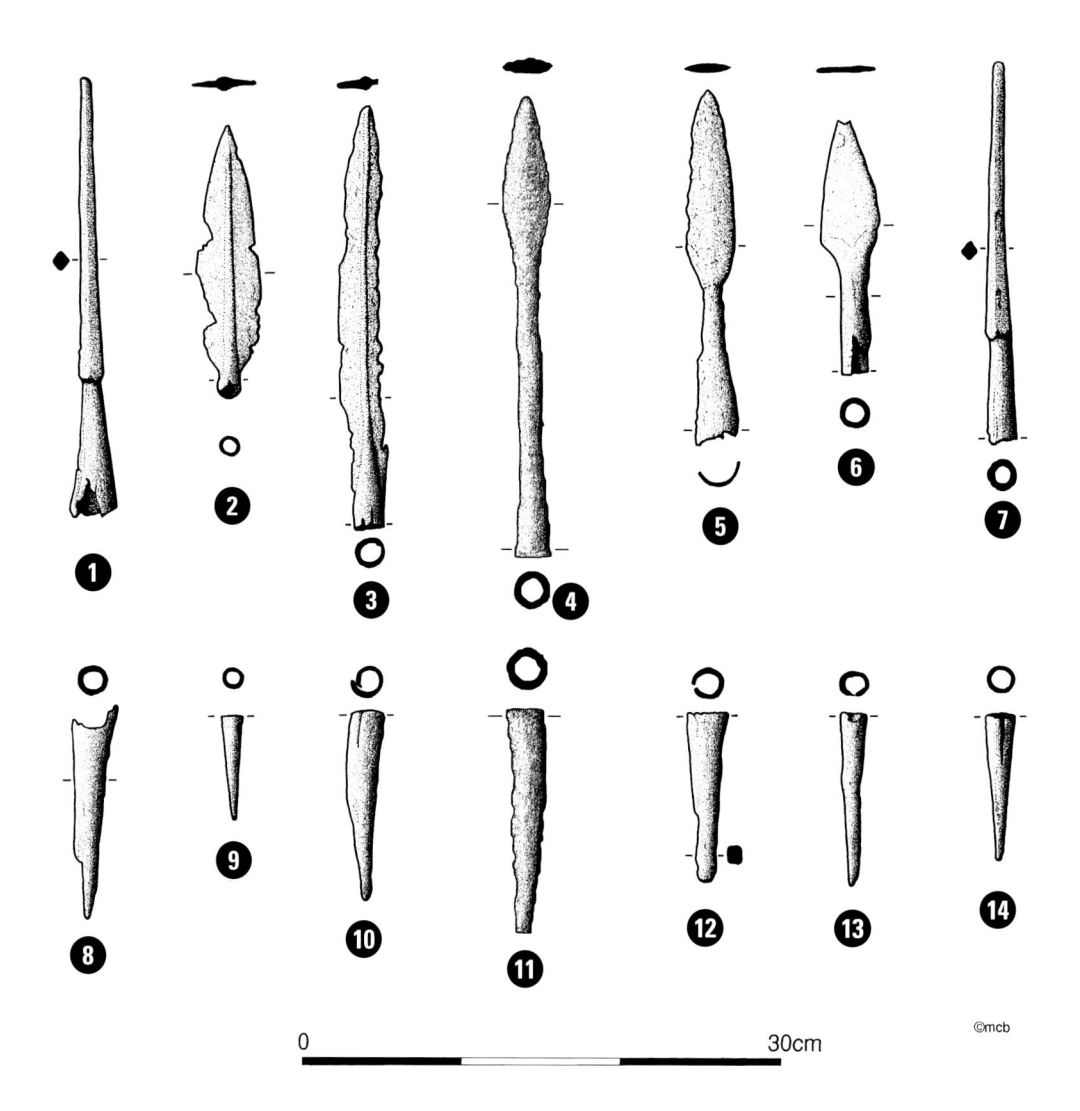

These drawings depict Republican spearheads and ferrules from Numantia (**1**, **2**, **6**, **7**, **9**, **13**, **14**), Cáceres (**3**, **5**, **8**, **10**, **12**) and Caminreal (**4**, **11**), all in Spain. Polybius describes the *pilum* thus: 'The wooden shaft of the javelin measures about two cubits [*c.*924mm] in length and is about a finger's breadth [*c.*19mm] in thickness; its head is a span [*c.*231mm] long hammered out to such a fine edge that it is necessarily bent by the first impact, and the enemy is unable to return it. If this were not so, the missile would be available for both sides' (6.22.4). (M.C. Bishop)

army they had at their disposal was the largest that Rome had ever fielded, but it had several shortcomings. It lacked experienced men, so many having been killed or fallen into captivity in the past 18 months. Moreover, the new recruits would likely have been levied from a broader base than was usual, perhaps with the suspension of the property qualification allowing many more men to become eligible for service (Healy 1994: 65), but they might not have the same level of military skill that many propertied recruits would already have attained before they even joined their legion. The new consuls were only elected in March, meaning that the legions they were raising had almost no time at all to train; this may have meant that standard legionary manoeuvres were too complex to perform for such callow troops, especially in the face of the enemy. The cavalry requirement from the *alae* had been doubled, but that still left a wide gap between the Roman and Carthaginian numbers, not to mention the fact that the Carthaginian force was proven and battle-hardened, which was the case with maybe only one-third of the Roman army's horsemen. Such factors must have been clear to both Roman commanders, and must in turn have influenced their decisions with regard to the eventual deployment of their army. Nevertheless they both seem to have lacked Hannibal's sense of strategic initiative, his appreciation of the fact that the easiest way to win a battle was to do it before one ever took to the battlefield. The decision of where and how to fight would be Hannibal's, not theirs.

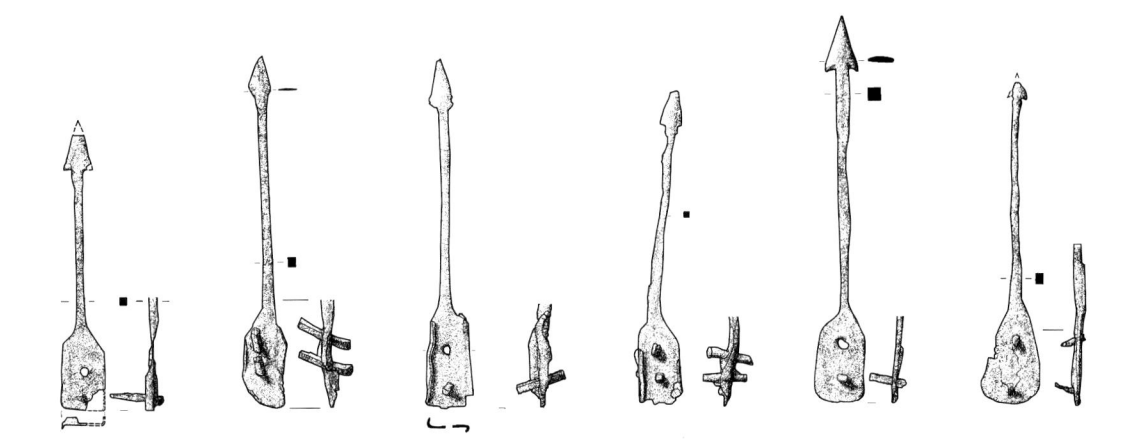

The new legions finally all came together around two days' march away from Cannae. Something like four months had passed since the new consuls had been elected, during which time they had doubled the size of the army and brought it into the field ready for battle, an astonishing feat of administrative and logistical skill. As the vast force began to move towards Hannibal's army, there was no doubt that both sides were not interested in any more evasions or strategic delays; each wanted the battle, and each hoped that it would be definitive.

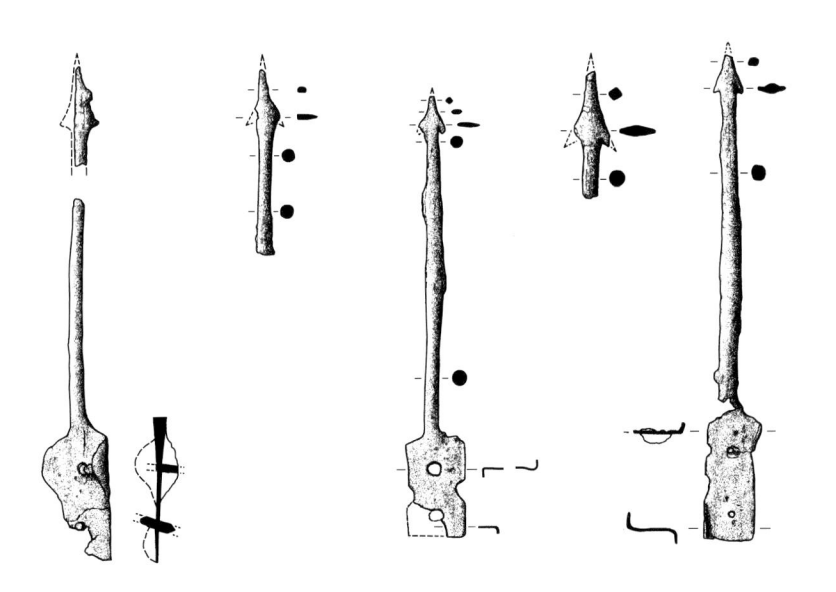

These drawings show (above) *pila* from Talamonaccio on the coast of Tuscany, central Italy, late 3rd century BC, and (below) *pila* from Castellruf, Spain, late 3rd century BC. It is difficult to be exact about the design and construction of the *pila* that legionaries used against Hannibal's armies, but the essential design – a thin iron shank seated in a wooden haft with square or flanged tangs – would be quite recognizable as the ancestor of those used in the Marian and later Imperial legions. Lighter javelins of a more straightforward socketed design were carried as well, possibly by *principes* and *hastati* in addition to their heavier *pila*, but certainly by the *velites*, for whom the lighter javelin was the main weapon. (MC. Bishop)

Cannae, 216 BC

MAP KEY

1 The Roman and Carthaginian armies have drawn up for battle at Cannae. After an inconclusive struggle between their respective light-infantry contingents, the Iberian and Gaulish cavalry of the left wing led by Hasdrubal charge the Roman cavalry opposite, overmastering them and routing them from the field.

2 The Roman legions advance, engaging with the Gaulish and Iberian infantry that make up Hannibal's main line, gradually forcing them back behind their original starting point. The Libyo-Phoenician heavy infantry positioned on both wings of the Carthaginian line turn inwards and attack both flanks of the Roman infantry.

3 The Numidian cavalry on the Carthaginian right wing charge at the Roman allied cavalry, engaging them. They are joined by Hasdrubal's returning cavalry, at which point the Roman allied cavalry flee, pursued by the Numidians.

4 Hasdrubal's cavalry turn on the rear of the Roman infantry line and launch repeated attacks. The Roman infantry, assailed from all sides, collapse and are destroyed.

Battlefield environment

At the time of the battle much of the ground was cultivated for wheat and other cereal crops, mostly grown in a patchwork of large fields, while smaller groves of olives and citrus trees also dotted the landscape. The modern town of San Ferdinando di Puglia was the probable location of Hannibal's main camp, with the Romans around 8km to the east. The Aufidius (known today as the Ofanto) was not a particularly large river, winding its way in a north-easterly direction towards the Adriatic Sea, but it was enough of an obstacle to make a safe anchor point for the Roman army's right wing. There is still some uncertainty as to the exact location of the battle, though it is most likely to have been fought on the wide plains to the east of the high ground on which the ruined citadel of Cannae sits. The day of battle was warm and dry, with the well-known local wind, the hot and dusty Volturnus, rising from the south around midday and blowing in the faces of the Romans, which, according to Livy, interfered with their sight and hampered their use of missile weapons while aiding the enemy in the use of theirs.

A view looking north-east over the plain of the Aufidius (Ofanto) River from the remains of the ancient town of Cannae; the ruined stone pillar that stands to the right was erected as a modern monument to the battle, and is located on the north-western edge of the site. The modern world has put its stamp on the area of the battle (located around 9–13km to the west of the coastal town of Barletta), which is crossed by roads, drainage ditches and the like, though much of the plain through which the Aufidius flowed remains agricultural, as it always was, with plentiful groves of olives and vineyards peppering the terrain. (Healy 1994: 91). The course of the Aufidius has changed over the centuries; at the time of the battle it was possibly closer to the higher ground where the modern town of San Ferdinando di Puglia now sits (located 6.5km to the west of the Cannae ruins, not shown in this image). (De Agostini/Getty Images)

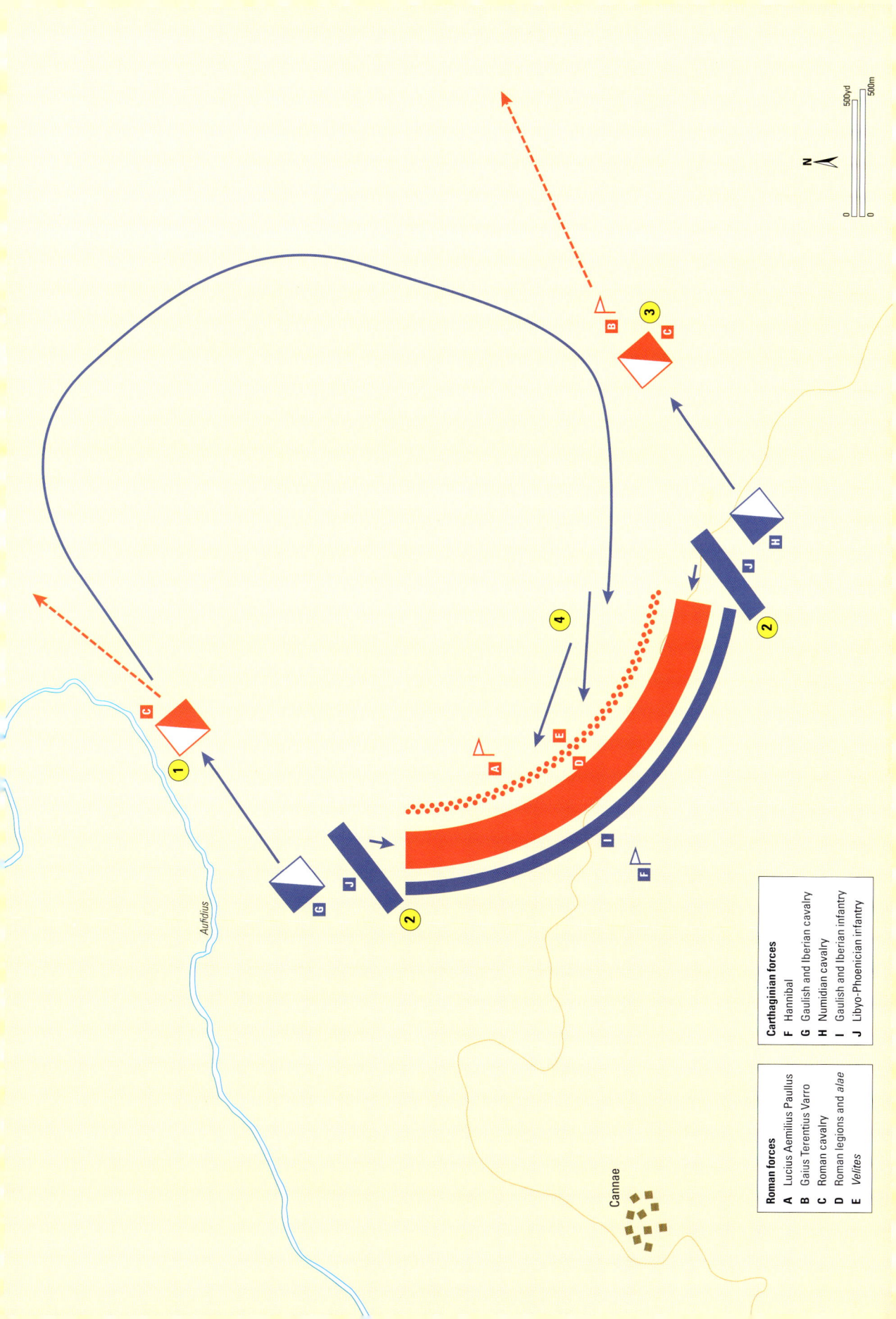

Roman forces

A Lucius Aemilius Paullus
B Gaius Terentius Varro
C Roman cavalry
D Roman legions and *alae*
E *Velites*

Carthaginian forces

F Hannibal
G Gaulish and Iberian cavalry
H Numidian cavalry
I Gaulish and Iberian infantry
J Libyo-Phoenician infantry

INTO COMBAT

The Roman force at Cannae likely numbered 80,000 infantry and 6,000 cavalry of whom 10,000 (one legion and one *ala*) were left to garrison the main camp, leaving a total force of around 76,000 to take to the field of battle (Daly 2002: 26–29). Polybius makes mention of the fact that many of the new recruits who filled out the new legions were raw levies, unused to the nature of legionary life and practice, and that they had never seen their enemy. All eight of the legions present were 5,300 men strong, 800 more than the usual full-strength mid-Republican legion. This was probably achieved by increasing the century from 60 to 72 men, each of the legions at Cannae therefore being made up of 300 cavalry, 1,520 *velites*, 1,440 *hastati*, 1,440 *principes* and 600 *triarii*. The allied legions were each 5,000 men strong, with a 600-man contingent of cavalry.

For Hannibal's army Polybius gives a total strength of 50,000 men (40,000 infantry and 10,000 cavalry), not counting a probable additional force of 8,000 Gauls who were the camp garrison and therefore did not take part in the battle. The heavy infantry was made up of around 10,000 Libyo-Phoenicians, 6,000 Iberians and 16,000 Gauls, while the light infantry numbered around 8,000 (made up of Balearian slingers and other light troops). There were 10,000 cavalry in total, probably 2,000 of whom were Iberian, 4,000 Gaulish and 4,000 Numidian (Daly 2002: 29–32). The Numidian horse were commanded by either Hanno (Polybius) or Maharbal (Livy). It is impossible to judge the accuracy of the numbers quoted by Polybius or Livy, but it does seem safe to assume that the Roman army outnumbered that of Hannibal by a reasonable degree, which would in part justify their eagerness for battle.

Eventually the combined Roman army came within sight of the Carthaginian position, setting up their own encampment 8km distant. Paullus was wary of the site, seeing the potential that the broad flat expanse held for cavalry action, but Varro disagreed, Polybius believes through inexperience. Shortly afterwards Varro overruled Paullus again, sending out a reconnaissance-in-force to get a better sense of Hannibal's position, but it was intercepted by a mixed detachment of cavalry and light infantry. Initially the Romans were thrown into confusion by the spoiling attack, but they reorganized their lines and drove the Carthaginians back, the skirmish developing into quite a fight that both sides had to abandon as night approached. The Carthaginians were discomfited by the Roman performance, but the following day Paullus, now in charge, refused to follow up with another incursion, instead splitting the army in two and setting up a new camp on the opposite side of the Aufidius River to protect the Roman foraging parties and threaten those of their enemy. Varro, no doubt, was less than pleased.

Hannibal knew that a battle was coming, and sought to reassure his men, gathering them round and giving a speech to remind them of all that they had achieved, pointing out that he did not need to make calls on their bravery as they had proven themselves on that score three times since they had crossed into Italia. A fragment of text from the poet Ennius (who lived through the war) has Hannibal exhorting his men to victory with the words: 'He who will strike a blow at the enemy – hear me! he will be a Carthaginian, whatever his name will be; whatever his country' (8.276–77). His encouragement had the desired effect, rousing the spirits of the camp in anticipation of the fight to come. The next day he established a second camp on the other side of the Aufidius, beginning the process of preparing his army for battle, but the Romans remained in their encampment; Paullus did not want to give battle in such a place and was intent on waiting Hannibal out, knowing that he would have to move soon as his supplies began to run out. Deciding that a bit of provocation was in order, Hannibal sent his Numidians out to harass the Romans as they tried to gather water, an action that enraged many Romans, including Varro.

At first light the following day Varro, in charge once more, drew the troops of both camps together on the southern bank of the Aufidius and arrayed them for battle angled southwards. The Roman horse he positioned on the right wing anchored by the river, followed by the infantry in a line that was narrower than usual, the spaces between the maniples being closed-up and the maniples themselves reducing their frontage and increasing their depth. The infantry was most likely arrayed in the four consular armies, advantageous for deployment, but due to the location of Varro and Paullus it meant that the two most inexperienced armies were on the flanks (Daly 2002: 156). The cavalry of the allies took up position on the left wing, while the *velites* and their allied equivalents came to the fore, screening the whole army. Paullus positioned himself on the Roman right wing with the cavalry, while Varro was on the left; Minucius and Servilius, the consuls of the previous year, were positioned in the centre with their armies.

In response, Hannibal detailed his 8,000 Balearian slingers and light spearmen across the river where they acted as a screen for the remainder of his army as it deployed opposite the Romans. On his left wing he positioned the Iberian and Gaulish horse (6,000–8,000 strong) under the command of a Carthaginian general called Hasdrubal, and next to them half his Libyo-Phoenician heavy infantry (5,000 strong); next came the Iberian *scutarii* interspersed with the Gauls (6,000 and 16,000 men respectively), then the other half of the Libyo-Phoenician heavy infantry (another 5,000 men); and finally on his right wing the Numidians (4,000 horsemen) led by Hanno, though Livy says Maharbal had the honour. Hannibal together with his brother Mago took up position in the centre of the Carthaginian line.

Hannibal gave the order to advance, his battle line conforming to the plan he had laid out for it; the Iberian *scutarii* and Gaulish infantry moved

A pair of bronze greaves, Etruscan, 4th century BC. In earlier centuries Carthaginian heavy infantry would have worn breastplates and greaves in much the same fashion as the Greeks, but by the time of the 3rd century BC it seems likely that most of them were wearing the *linothorax* (a cuirass with shoulder-doubling made from layers of glued linen) as their main form of protection, though still with bronze greaves (Salimbeti & D'Amato 2014: 32). The fact that these troops stripped the Roman dead of their *loricae hamatae* after the Trebia and Lake Trasimene is a further indication that they wore *linothorax* armour, as it would be unlikely for a man possessed of a bronze breastplate to relinquish it in favour of a coat of mail. (Metropolitan Museum of Art, www.metmuseum.org)

A Roman republican legionary re-enactor pausing for refreshment on a route march. Ancient accounts together with the results of modern re-enactment and analysis suggest that in battle, Roman lines were not tightly packed, giving legionaries space to fight and manoeuvre effectively. When in line a legionary would take up around 0.8–1m of frontage (Daly 2002: 158–60), and he had room behind him too, with enough space between the ranks to allow for the degree of movement required to cast his *pilum*. At Cannae, as the Roman lines were forced back upon one another, such room to manoeuvre and fight would have become increasingly constricted, and was a probable factor in the transformation of the battle into a massacre. (DEA/C. BALOSSINI/ De Agostini/Getty Images)

forwards in a shallow echelon, the central units in the lead, with those either side of them staggered back towards the flanks and creating a line in the shape of a crescent, diminishing in depth towards the edges. Polybius notes how strange the line looked as it advanced, the Iberians in their short linen tunics edged in purple next to the rough, wild-looking Gauls, many of them probably shirtless, all behind their wall of large oval shields. The battle began as the two bodies of light troops, the *velites* of legions in concert with their equivalents from the allies on one side, confronted by Balearian slingers and Iberian *caetrati* from the other, closed against one another, the struggle quickly devolving into a series of messy and inconclusive skirmishes as such engagements often did.

Such skirmishes soon gave way to something much more serious as the Gaulish and Iberian cavalry on the Carthaginian left were unleashed in 'true barbaric fashion' (Polybius 3.115), charging along the southern bank of the Aufidius until they crashed head-on into the Roman *equites*. The ground was narrow, with the river to one side and solid walls of infantry to the other, channelling the battle into a confined space that allowed no room for either side to manoeuvre; there were none of the usual niceties of such an engagement with bodies of horse feinting and riding away from one another, or trying to ride around each other's flanks, the situation forcing them to attack each other face to face. The action quickly descended into a vicious mêlée of hand-to-hand combat, the two forces grappling with one another as the quarters were so close that the horses were practically standing still next to each other, their riders wrestling one another off their mounts and continuing to fight on foot. The Romans resisted well and with vigour, but they were soon overmatched by the violence of the action and suffered many dead, finally breaking and riding headlong back along the river, the Carthaginians in hot pursuit and giving them no quarter.

As the Roman right wing began to disintegrate under this onslaught, the heavy infantry of the legions moved into action, marching into contact with the Iberians and Gauls of the Carthaginian centre. Paullus, having survived the onslaught, escaped from the pursuit with a small mounted bodyguard and rode to the centre of the Roman infantry line where he thought he could do the most good as it was clear that the day would be decided by the legionaries, and began encouraging his men in their exertions, much as Hannibal was doing on the opposite side. The Punic line staved off the initial Roman assault, fighting well and holding its own for a short time, but soon the disparity between the two sides started to tell. The Iberians and Gauls were spread thinly, their lines lacking depth, whereas the legions opposing them were densely packed, soon becoming even more so as the Carthaginian line started to buckle and fall back. The Romans pushed forwards, the flanks of the infantry line (Paullus' and Varro's inexperienced men, perhaps overeager to be a part of the final victory) contracting inwards to add their weight to the great central thrust that was hammering into the centre of Hannibal's main line. Scenting victory the maniples pushed harder, driving the Gauls further backwards, the resistance crumbling in the face of a giant Roman wedge that had turned a convex line into a concave one.

By constant pressure the legions were able to push deep into the retreating Carthaginian centre, advancing to the point where the flanks of the Roman main line were now level with the Libyo-Phoenician heavy infantry that had been positioned on the wings of the Gauls and Iberians. The Libyo-Phoenician wings wheeled inwards and charged, crashing into both flanks of the Roman line simultaneously. The legionaries, at first flushed with the prospect of victory, realized that they suddenly had another, more serious battle to fight. What was more, their lines were tired from the exertion of battling the Gauls and Iberians, but now they faced fresh, eager enemy troops. The flanks of the Roman lines must have realigned themselves as best they could, though any such manoeuvring would surely have been extremely difficult as they were still engaged to the front, their ranks had been even further constricted by the nature of their advance, and the simultaneous attacks by the Libyo-Phoenicians would have denied them the chance to do much more than form impromptu lines of defence to fend off the initial charge. In addition the shock of receiving attacks in both flanks would likely have knocked the impetus out of the Roman front ranks who had been advancing steadily against the retreating Gauls and Iberians, giving those troops time to breathe and regroup before closing with a now-presumably discomfited Roman battle line.

As the Roman infantry was dealing with this unanticipated crisis the Numidian horse now made their move, charging at the Roman cavalry on the left wing that was commanded by Varro, where despite the fact that 'from the peculiar nature of their mode of fighting, they neither inflicted nor received much harm, they yet rendered the enemy's horse useless by keeping them occupied, and charging them first on one side and then on another' (Polybius 3.116). It is possible that the allied cavalry could have eventually brushed the Numidians aside, but they were soon reinforced by Hasdrubal and his Gaulish and Iberian horsemen, fresh from the bloody

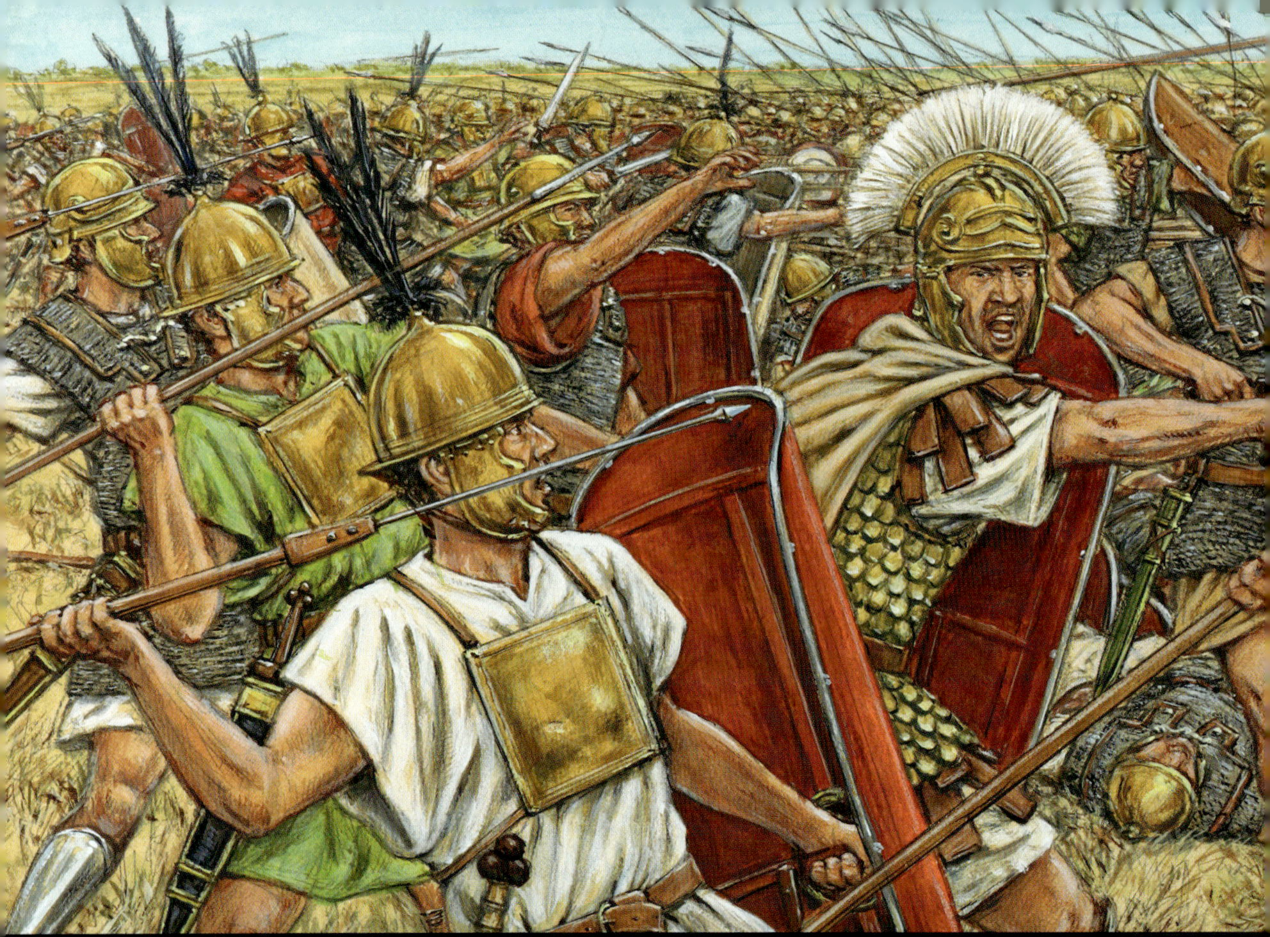

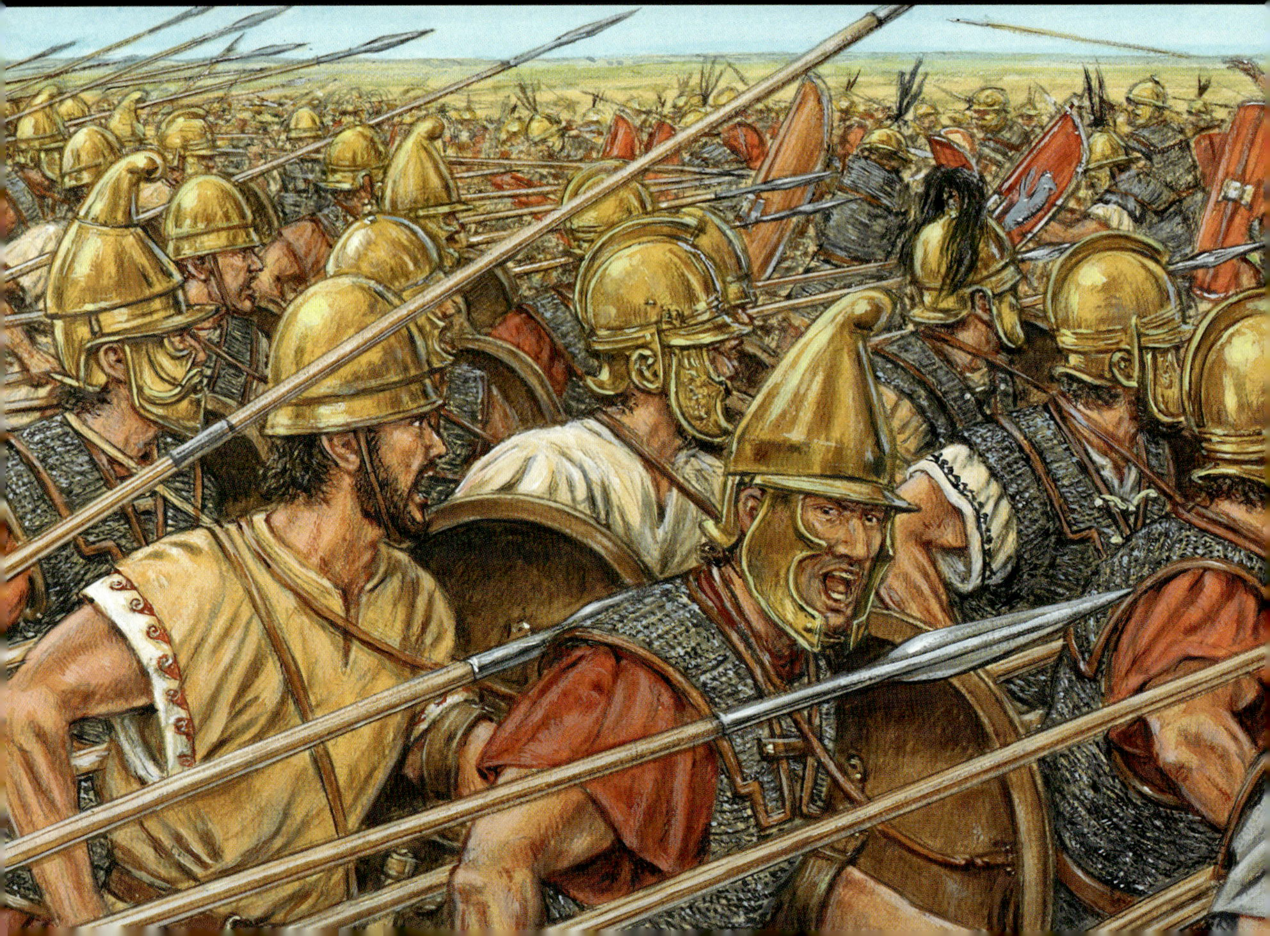

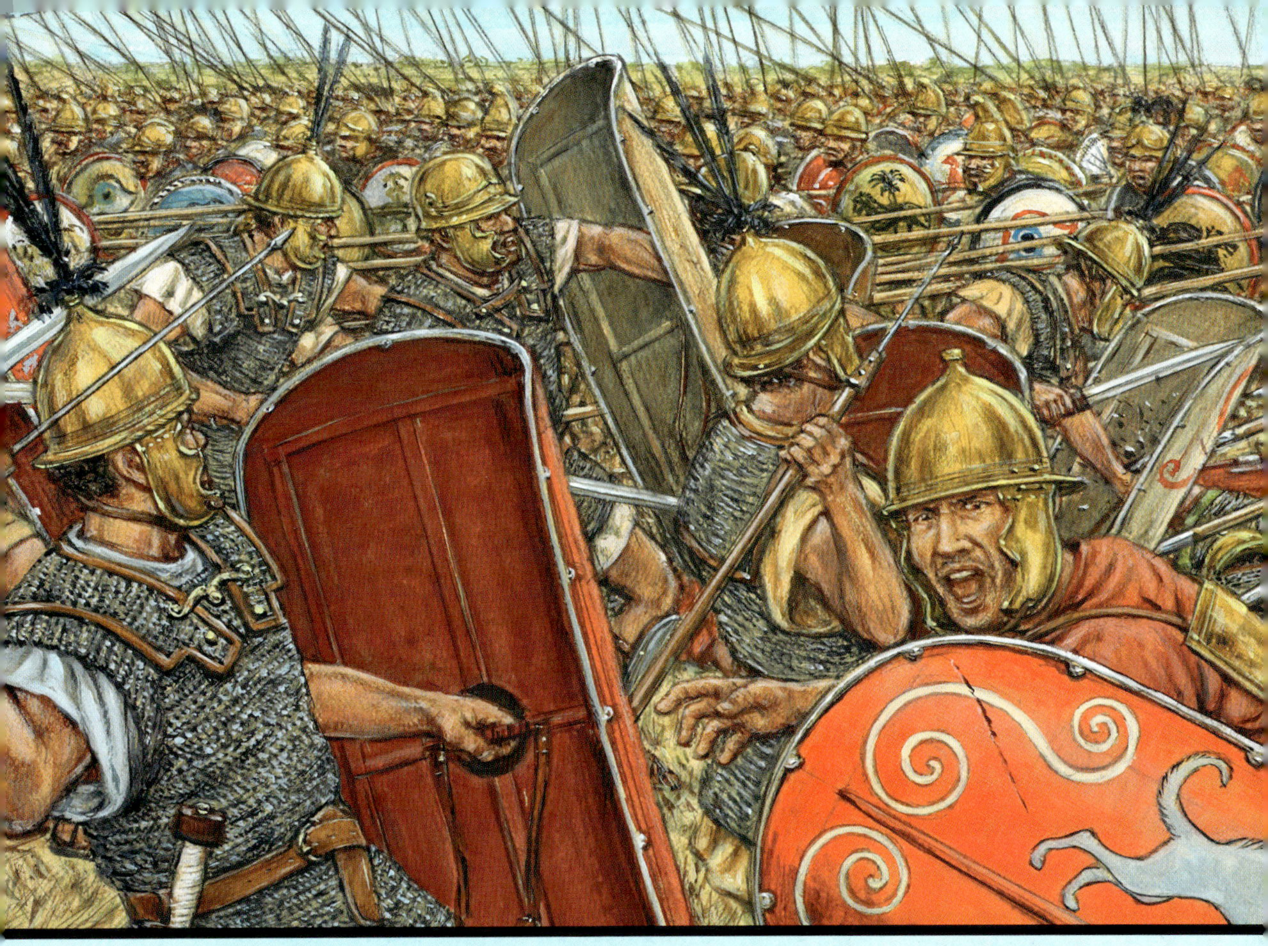
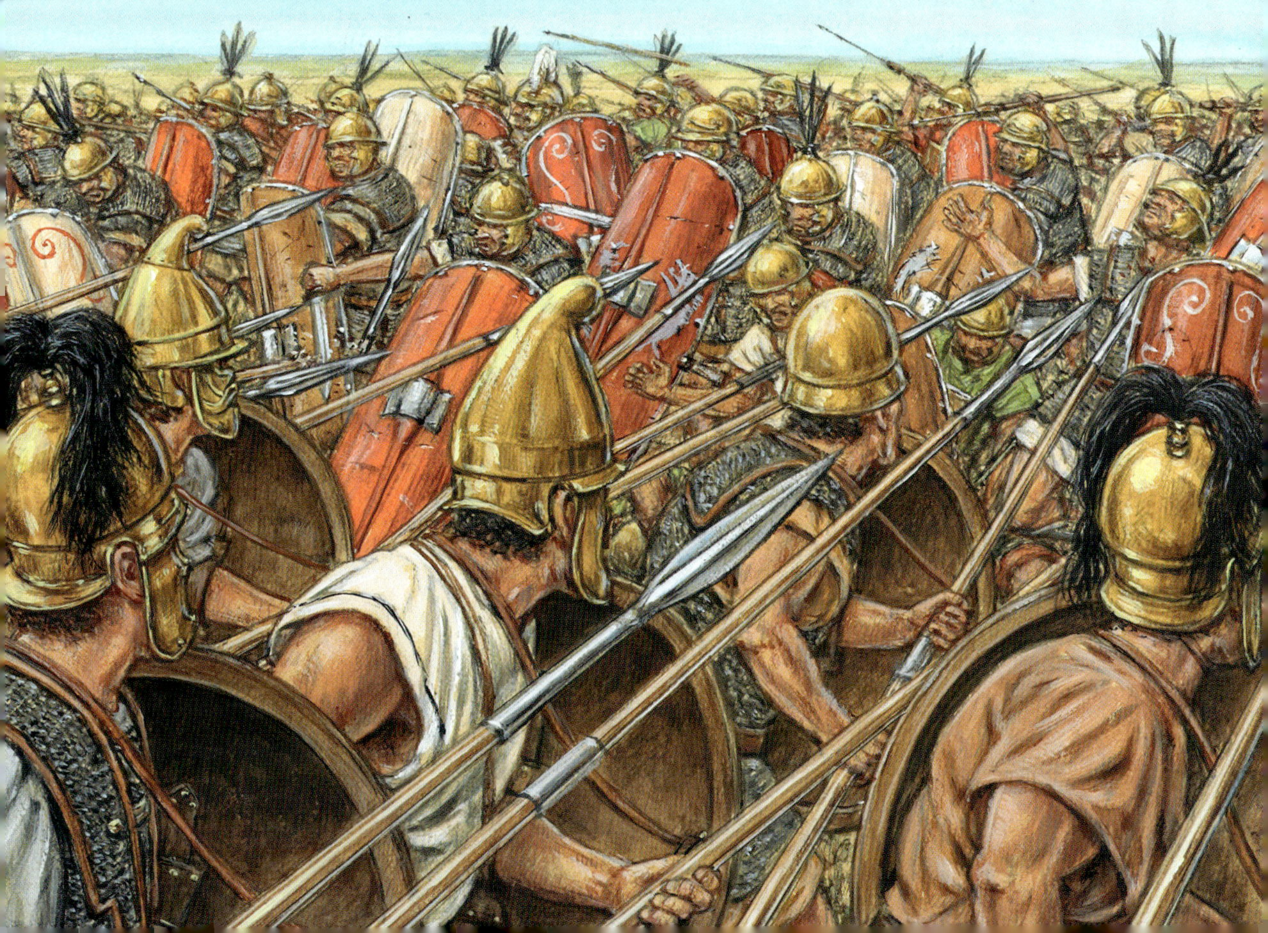

The legions under pressure

Roman view: The flanks of the Roman battle line have been overwhelmed by the determined attacks of Hannibal's Libyo-Phoenician phalanxes. The Roman lines have become disordered by the crush of combat, the maniples of *hastati* and *principes* now intermingled in the confusion, denying the Romans the space they need to manoeuvre and re-form if they are to maintain an effective defence. Despite the critical position of the legionaries they are still fighting back as best they can; much of their morale comes from the example of a bold centurion who exhorts the men around him to keep their nerve in the face of imminent disaster. The Libyo-Phoenicians are pressing forward over ground increasingly littered with Roman dead and dying, cut down where they stood and left where they fell; the mixed lines of *hastati* and *principes* are beginning to disintegrate as their maniples and those stacked up behind them are forced ever further backwards. With Carthaginian troops now on all sides such a retreat has nowhere to go, however, and will drive the legionaries into ever-tighter groups that give each man precious little space to fight, and no space at all to flee.

Carthaginian view: The initial attack by the legions drove into Hannibal's battle line, engaging it along its length and hammering at the Celtic and Iberian troops that defended the Carthaginian centre. Roman determination looked to be rewarded as the Carthaginians started to retreat, slowly at first then faster. But then, at the height of the Roman advance, the Carthaginian line stiffened, while the allied legions on both flanks buckled under sudden assaults by Libyo-Phoenician phalanxes. Confusion turns to panic as sweeping attacks by Carthaginian cavalry on the rear of the Roman line box the legions in, their room to manoeuvre vanishing before they can do anything to stop it. Hannibal's fist slowly tightens around the Roman battle line, which begins to disintegrate. The Libyo-Phoenician phalangites, many armoured in Roman mail shirts stripped from their enemy dead at Lake Trasimene the previous year, advance steadily, the bristling wall of their *sarissae* forcing back or killing all in their path. A confused mass of legionaries face oncoming Libyo-Phoenicians who already seem to be exulting in the victory that will so soon be theirs, their *sarissae* lowered as they advance to finish their bloody job.

execution they had committed on the rest of the Roman cavalry by the river. Faced with such odds, the allied horse broke and ran. Hasdrubal, thinking quickly, set the Numidians after the retreating allied cavalry to harry them from the field, while he pulled his own cavalry together and made for the infantry battle to support the Libyo-Phoenicians. The loss of the remainder of the Roman allied cavalry was a serious blow, as such a force could have made a significant difference to the travails of the infantry if it had been able to attack one of the Libyo-Phoenician wings. As it was their flight, understandable as it may have been in the face of such large numbers of enemy cavalry, left the Roman infantry to fend for themselves.

The Roman legions and their allies were in desperate trouble. The arrival of Hasdrubal was another hammer-blow, his cavalry charging into the rear of the Roman line (which had presumably turned outwards to receive such assaults), launching a series of rolling attacks with squadron after squadron hitting all along the length of the line, causing havoc and confusion among the Roman ranks, encouragement and elation among those of the Libyo-Phoenicians. It is likely that the Carthaginian cavalry fell upon the disordered and lightly armed ranks of *velites*, who would have fallen back through the main line and re-formed at the rear, unwittingly becoming a perfect target for Hasdrubal's depredations (Daly 2002: 193).

The legions still held, perhaps in part due to the examples of their tribunes, Servilius and of Paullus, the fate of whom Livy recounts in some (perhaps embellished) detail. Early in the battle Paullus had been seriously wounded by a sling stone, but despite that he did his best to shore up the lines of the legions, stiffening resolve and averting disaster when it threatened. Finally too weak to stay on his horse he dismounted along with his retinue, who endured the wrath of the Carthaginians, frustrated that these men continued to fight on even though their situation was obviously hopeless. The consul's retinue were gradually cut down, the few remaining survivors dragging their exhausted and badly wounded bodies back onto their horses if they could in an effort to escape, but Paullus remained, overwhelmed and killed by a band of Carthaginians who did not even realize who he was. Servilius too fell about this time, Appian noting that upon the death of those two generals Roman morale started to crack, with men beginning the task of trying to fight their way out.

As long as the legions could maintain some sort of coherent front, even if that front was now on all four sides, they could hang together and keep the enemy at bay, but that became more and more difficult to sustain as the outer ranks were continually losing men, with those remaining becoming ever more battered and compressed. In addition it is likely that this great mass of men was being showered with javelins and sling stones from the Carthaginian light infantry, causing casualties, confusion and frustration at the Romans' inability to do anything to defend themselves against such attacks. At some point Roman cohesion must have started to unravel as different units were forced in on one another; officers could call out orders, but their legionaries would have been physically unable to comply, the increasing crush denying them any sort of chance to deploy or manoeuvre, quarters probably becoming so close that they could not even raise their swords to fight. In such a situation eventually panic and despair would have overwhelmed many, but they could not even flee, hemmed-in as they were. Individuals and small groups would have continued to fight, no doubt, but by this stage it could not change the outcome, Polybius recounting that 'at last were all killed on the field' (3.116).

The cost in lives lost was terrible, Livy recounting the scene of the battlefield the day after:

> So many thousands of Romans were lying, foot and horse promiscuously, according as accident had brought them together, either in the battle or in the flight. Some, whom their wounds, pinched by the morning cold, had roused, as they were rising up, covered with blood, from the midst of the heaps of slain, were overpowered by the enemy. Some too they found lying alive with their thighs and hams cut, who, laying bare their necks and throats, bid them drain the blood that remained in them. (22.51.6–7)

As well as the consul Aemilius Paullus, Marcus Atilius and Gnaeus Servilius Geminus, the consuls of the previous year, were both killed, together with 29 tribunes, at least 80 men of senatorial rank (or who had senatorial prospects) who had chosen to go along and fight with the legions, and hundreds of *equites*.

The vast majority of the Roman cavalry was lost, some 300 or so escaping the depredations of Hasdrubal and the pursuit of the Numidians, while for the infantry only 3,000 of those engaged on the field of battle survived, escaping to surrounding towns and villages, the rest dying on the field. The contingent that Paullus had left to guard the camp was quickly buttoned up by Hannibal in the immediate aftermath of the battle, some 2,000 being killed and the rest going into captivity. Polybius gives the total Roman dead at around 70,000, though Livy is likely more accurate with his estimate of 45,500 foot and 2,700 horse dead, 19,300 captured and 14,550 escaped. Varro, commanding the allied cavalry on the left wing, had broken and fled with the rest when they were threatened with being overwhelmed by Hasdrubal. The pursuing Numidians caused great losses among the fleeing horsemen, but Varro was not among them, eventually making it with some 70 others to Venusia (Venosa). Polybius was damning, describing the shame of Varro's fight as being as big a disgrace to his honour as his conduct in office had been calamitous for his country.

For Hannibal, the victory was nearly perfect. His losses were acceptable (especially considering the scale of his victory), with Polybius citing 5,700 dead and Livy 8,000 dead. Once again he had sought a battle on his terms, and his enemy had obliged him. The destruction of eight legions and their *alae* was a massive blow to Roman military power and prestige, a blow so great in fact, that it was reasonable to wonder if it could prove fatal. Hannibal's officers suggested that he and the army should rest after so great a success, but his cavalry commander Maharbal disagreed, saying he should lose no time in moving on Rome itself; he would ride ahead, arriving in the city before they even realized he was on his way. Hannibal, full of joy at his victory, applauded Maharbal's zeal but equivocated over the course of action he suggested. Maharbal replied, rather pointedly, 'You know how to conquer, Hannibal; but you do not know how to make use of your victory' (quoted in Livy 22.51.4).

Ilipa

206 BC

BACKGROUND TO BATTLE

Iberia had become a graveyard of Roman ambition since the start of the war against Hannibal. The nominal cause of the conflict was the treatment of the town of Saguntum, an ally of Rome located on the Iberian Mediterranean coast, which was besieged and eventually captured by Hannibal in 219 BC, as part of his consolidation of his base of operations prior to his invasion of Italia. Even without the Carthaginian presence it would have been a difficult land to manage, split as it was between a number of warring, fractious tribes who could, in the old adage, be rented for a time, but never really bought. It was not just the home of truculent local warlords, though, but of the resurgent Carthaginian empire, marked by the founding of Carthago Nova (New Carthage;

A Celtiberian dagger in the remains of its iron-framed sheath, Museo Arqueológico Nacional (National Archaeological Museum) in Madrid. The design is similar in some respects to the Roman *pugio* (which evolved from Celtic dagger designs), but its distinctive 'antennae' mark it out as a Celtic piece. (Prisma/UIG via Getty Images)

modern-day Cartagena) in 228 BC by Hasdrubal the Fair. In the wake of their defeat in the First Punic War, the Carthaginians (in the shape of Hamilcar Barca and his sons, Hannibal, Hasdrubal and Mago) brought much of Iberia under their heel; the new province proved to be a strategic asset of significant importance, providing plentiful silver from its mines and many warlike men from its various tribes, both of which would be crucial in the prosecution of a much-wanted new war against Rome. Iberia also offered a jumping-off point for overland campaigns against Rome, now a necessity since Carthaginian sea power had never recovered from the battering it had taken from the Romans in the previous war.

After Hannibal had launched his invasion of Italia it became clear that curtailing his ability to receive funds and reinforcements from Iberia would severely hamper his attempts to destroy Roman power, and to that end several attempts were made to wrest control of the province from Carthage; all proved failures to varying degrees, often resulting in military defeat, death and occasional ignominy. Despite such reverses, Roman persistence did make it more difficult for the Carthaginians to provide Hannibal with the men and *matériel* he needed, their campaigns forcing valuable resources to be spent in Iberia rather than Italia. Into this arena in 210 BC came Publius Cornelius Scipio, who in being appointed to the Iberian command may, in the eyes of some in Rome, have been taking on something of a poisoned chalice. His task – to break Punic power in Iberia, and destroy or expel all their armies – was significant, and was not helped by the fact that Roman expeditions had often been dogged by poor supplies and infrequent drafts of reinforcements, both factors which exacerbated the difficulties inherent in campaigning in a foreign land.

Though only 24 years old, the Young Scipio was no stranger to the battlefield, having been at Ticinus and the Trebia, possibly also at Lake Trasimene, as well as surviving the catastrophe of Cannae, and he quickly proved to be a potent enemy for Punic forces in Iberia. Described by Polybius as 'a man eminently careful, acute, and prompt' (11.25), he was a scion of the Cornelii Scipiones, a well-established patrician family that had already seen several of its members heavily involved in the war against Hannibal in general, and in Iberia in particular; Gnaeus Cornelius Scipio Calvus ('the bald', his uncle) and Publius Cornelius Scipio (his father) had both been killed in the Roman defeat at the Battle of the Upper Baetis in 211 BC, by an army under the command of Hasdrubal Gisco. Scipio's first act was dramatic – a surprise march to capture Carthago Nova in 209 BC, a severe blow to Punic pride, as well as a political boon for Scipio in the form of the Iberian hostages that fell into his hands, allowing him to make significant inroads in negotiations with the important tribes of the region. Scipio followed this in 208 BC by moving on Hasdrubal Barca's army at Baecula (Santo Tomé), forcing him from a well-prepared defensive position that demonstrated once again Scipio's tactical acumen and confidence. His victory over Hasdrubal Barca was not significant strategically, but it buttressed his growing reputation among some of the Iberian tribes, making it easier for him to win their support.

Command of the Carthaginian armies in Iberia fell to Hasdrubal Gisco at Gades (Cádiz) and Mago Barca at Cástulo, a town upriver on the Baetis in south-central Iberia. (Hasdrubal Barca had also had an army in the peninsula, but his death at the Metaurus in 207 BC left Iberia in the hands of Gisco and Mago.) Hasdrubal Gisco, described by Livy as 'the greatest and most renowned general concerned in the war, next to the Barcine family' (28.12), was a highly experienced general who had enjoyed genuine victories over the Romans, and who also possessed the political skills that were an essential part of Carthaginian high command, as the recruitment and management of Punic armies depended in large part on a mixture of alliances, treaties, bribes and threats.

The year 207 BC saw Hasdrubal Gisco consolidating his positions throughout southern Iberia, while Scipio indulged in some frustrating incursions that came to naught because Hasdrubal Gisco refused to march out onto the field of battle and fight. Hasdrubal Barca, after his defeat at Baecula, had moved his army over the Alps into Italia in an attempt to reinforce his brother Hannibal, but had come to grief at the Battle of the Metaurus, dashing Carthaginian hopes of a decisive victory on Rome's doorstep. With Hasdrubal Barca's failure it became necessary to make short work of Scipio if Hannibal was to be once again reinforced and resupplied from the Carthaginian forces in Iberia. As the year turned, Hasdrubal Gisco took the initiative and moved out of his winter quarters at Gades, assembling a significant force with which he intended to overwhelm the Roman upstart, an endeavour which also drew in Mago Barca (Hannibal's youngest brother) in support. Hasdrubal moved his army into the field, marching northwards until eventually coming to rest a little way past the town of Ilipa (Alcalá del Río) where he made camp on a hillside, digging a defensive entrenchment at the foot of the slope that gave out onto a broad plain 'well suited for a contest and battle' (Polybius 11.20).

A line of re-enactors' republican legionary *scuta*. The Roman *scutum* gave the bearer significant personal protection, and almost certainly had a tactical role in the way that legionaries en masse were deployed and expected to fight, though this was unlikely to have included the traditional 'pushing match' that was a characteristic of the older hoplite phalanxes. Roman ranks were spaced to allow for the casting of *pila*, whereas a phalanx depended on succeeding ranks being able to close up on one another, adding to the forward momentum of the front line's 'push' against their opponents. The *scutum*'s weight and heavy iron boss made it a useful offensive weapon too, particularly when used in conjunction with the *gladius*. (DEA/C. BALOSSINI/De Agostini/Getty Images)

Ilipa, 206 BC

MAP KEY

1 The Carthaginian army, caught off-guard by harassing Roman attacks, forms up with great haste in the same deployment that it has used on each of the preceding days.

2 Scipio's Roman legions, positioned on the flanks of his Iberian allies who form the centre of his line, manoeuvre towards the opposing Carthaginian flanks.

3 Roman legions crash into Hasdrubal Gisco's Iberians while Roman cavalry and *velites* simultaneously envelop both the left and right Carthaginian flanks, causing havoc among the elephants and destabilizing the entire Punic line.

4 Hasdrubal's Carthaginians are forced back, slowly at first and then in a rout, towards their encampment in the hills. The Roman pursuit is abandoned due to a fortuitous thunderstorm.

Battlefield environment

The site of the battle was bounded on one side by a winding ridge of high ground which ran from Ilipa (the modern town of Alcalá del Río) in a north-easterly direction, and on the other by the course of the Baetis River (the modern Guadalquivir) which followed a roughly parallel north-easterly path to the hills. The Punic camp was located on a spur of the high ground, within sight of the similarly situated Roman camp a little further away to the north-east. The low-lying area where battle was joined would likely have been a mix of farmland and rough ground, though it is impossible to be precise as to the exact nature of the terrain after so many centuries.

A view of the plains to the east of Esquivel, a modern village 4.5km north-east of Alcalá del Río (ancient Ilipa) in southern Spain. The site of the battle has been the source of some conjecture over the years, but this location is a reasonable prospect due to topographical consistency with the ancient sources (pointed out by the classical scholar H.H. Scullard in the 1930s, augmented by the work of later historians), as well as the fact that it is the only reasonably flat area in the vicinity of the ancient site of Ilipa and the Baetis (Guadalquivir) River that could accommodate an encounter between two armies of such significant size. (Courtesy of Marje and Vincent van Bijnen, www.the-romans.eu)

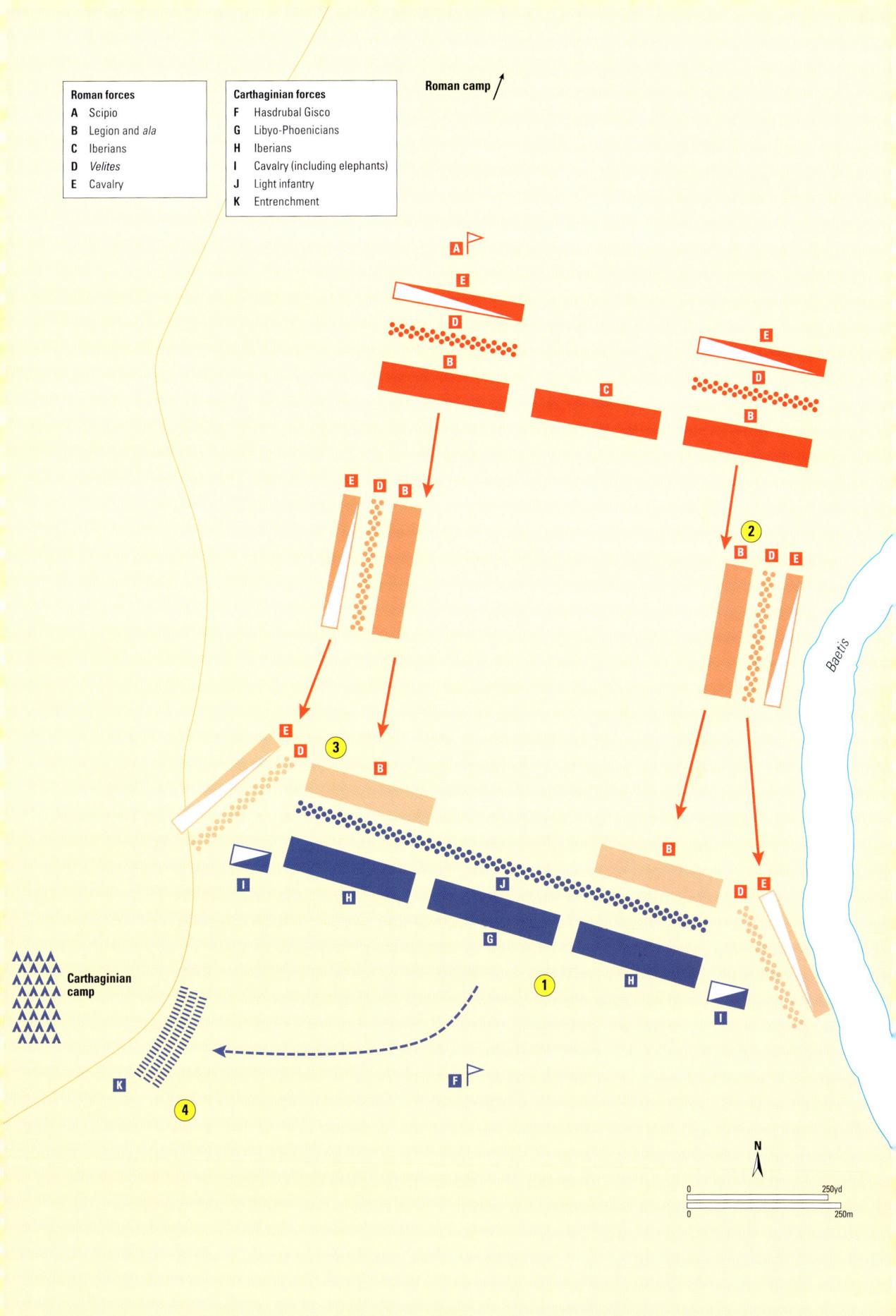

Roman forces
A Scipio
B Legion and *ala*
C Iberians
D *Velites*
E Cavalry

Carthaginian forces
F Hasdrubal Gisco
G Libyo-Phoenicians
H Iberians
I Cavalry (including elephants)
J Light infantry
K Entrenchment

Roman camp

Baetis

Carthaginian camp

N

0   250yd
0   250m

INTO COMBAT

As always, the exact number of troops in attendance at an ancient battle is difficult to establish with any certainty; for the Carthaginians, Polybius cites 74,000 men (70,000 infantry, 4,000 cavalry) as well as 32 elephants (Appian says 36), Livy a perhaps more reasonable 54,500 (50,000 infantry, 4,500 cavalry). At the heart of Hasdrubal's force were his Libyo-Phoenician heavy infantry, but he also had considerable numbers of levies that had been drawn from across the Iberian Peninsula, organized and brought to him by Mago Barca. In addition he enjoyed the support of his Iberian allies, including what was most likely a sizeable contingent of the dominant local tribe, the Turdetani, under the leadership of their prince Attanes. The Iberians had heavy-infantry (*scutarii*) spearmen protected by varying levels of personal armour as well as the large oval shields common to Celto-Iberian cultures, and light infantry (*caetrati*) who wore little or no armour, protected only by their *caetrae*, and armed with throwing spears (simple javelins of the usual sort as well as the Iberian *saunion* – a long, thin all-iron javelin that the Romans called the *soliferrum*). Also under Hasdrubal's command was the excellent North African cavalry leader Masinissa, together with his renowned and experienced Numidian horsemen, and possibly some Balearian mercenaries as well, acting as slingers and light infantry.

For Scipio the army of Romans and allies came to 45,000 infantry and 3,000 cavalry, around half of the total force being the two Roman legions and their two accompanying *alae*, the remainder being made up of Iberian allied tribes. Though his relations with several of the local tribes were very good (they had provided him with important support in his campaigns that led to the victory at Baecula), Scipio well remembered the fact that his father and uncle had relied upon similar alliances only to see their 'allies' bought out from under them by Hasdrubal Gisco, a betrayal that severely weakened the Roman position and soon led to the deaths of both Romans. Scipio needed the Iberians, because without them he had no hope of victory in battle against Hasdrubal's larger force, and yet it would be too great a gamble to rest his hopes of success on such potentially untrustworthy ground. It seems certain that Scipio's attitude to his local allies played a large part in determining his tactics when it came to facing Hasdrubal.

Gathering his forces to him as he went, Scipio moved his whole army towards Hasdrubal's camp, pitching his own camp on a hill opposite that of his enemy. Mago Barca, observing the Romans and their allies as they went about the business of setting up their camp, thought that such activity offered an excellent opportunity for an attack. Mago took the bulk of his cavalry and, in concert with Masinissa and his Numidians, rode for the Roman camp in the expectation of catching Scipio off-guard. Anticipating such a ploy, Scipio had positioned a covering force of cavalry of a similar size in the dead ground between the hills, allowing them to charge the Carthaginian horsemen in the flank as they approached the camp. The result was initial confusion, with a significant part of Mago's force routed immediately and riding back to their own camp, but a proportion of them closed with the Romans and began a fierce engagement. They were surprised to find themselves overmatched by the Roman horsemen who were soon reinforced by light infantry from the

A representation of Masinissa (*c*.238–148 BC), the commander of the Numidian horse at Ilipa. He was described by Polybius, who knew him personally, as 'the best man of all the kings of our time, and the most completely fortunate' (37.10). He had a long and eventful life, the earlier part of which saw him heavily involved in the Second Punic War, initially as a feared and talented Carthaginian cavalry commander in Iberia (he was betrothed to Hasdrubal Gisco's daughter), and later (after 206 BC) as a firm ally to the Romans, in whose cause he fought at Zama. After the war he was rewarded with the kingship of Numidia, enjoying a long life and dying peacefully at the age of 90. (Numidix/Wikimedia/CC BY-SA 3.0)

OPPOSITE
A 2nd-century BC marble bust of Scipio Africanus. Publius Cornelius Scipio Africanus (236–183 BC) was an extraordinary man who cultivated an image of martial virtue as well as one of cultural depth. His appointment to the Iberian command was unique, as no such post had ever been gifted to a man who had not held public office, and his success there saw him elected consul in 205 BC. The Roman invasion of Africa – an act that would lead to the eventual defeat of Hannibal at Zama in 202 BC, resulting in the surrender of Carthage – was undertaken on his initiative, and earned him the cognomen 'Africanus'. (DEA / G. DAGLI ORTI/De Agostini/Getty Images)

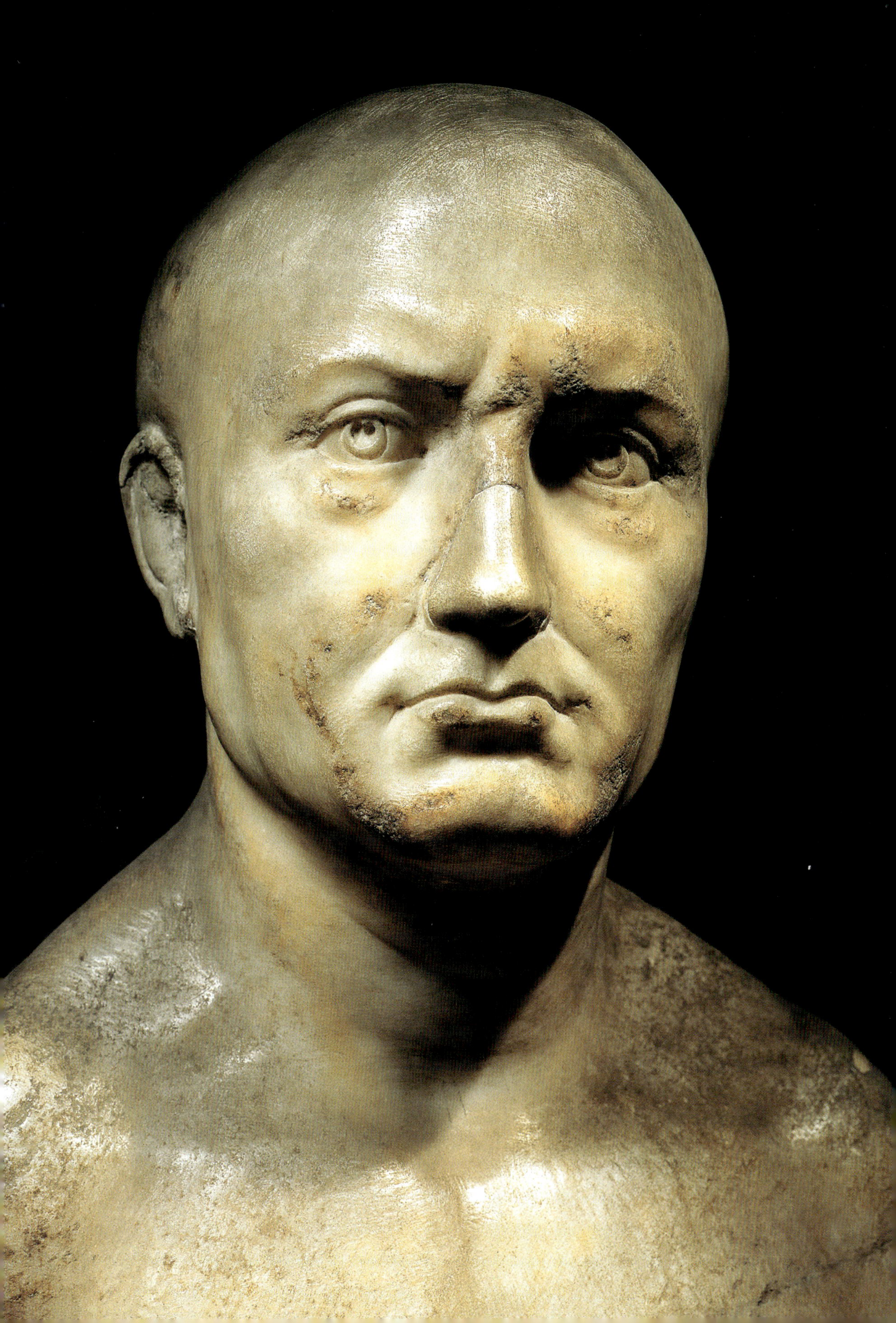

outposts as well as a quickly formed body of legionaries from the encampment, and soon began to fall back, first in an orderly fashion, and then, close-pressed by the aggressive Roman cavalry, in a pell-mell riot of disorder, many of them falling before the remainder gained the safety of their own ground. Though little more than a skirmish in the grand scheme of things, the victory was an important fillip to Roman morale, especially considering the reputation of Carthaginian cavalry in general and Masinissa's Numidians in particular.

Such skirmishes between Roman and Carthaginian cavalry and light infantry set the pattern for the next few days, which saw a continuous series of encounters but no decisive actions other than the chance for individuals or bodies of troops to test their mettle against the enemy, a popular pastime in an age when personal glory on the field of battle mattered a great deal. Eventually those inconclusive rigmaroles gave way to a significant demonstration of force by Hasdrubal, who moved his whole army down from his encampment, past his entrenchments and onto the plain where they were drawn up for battle. Scipio, moving off a little later in response, matched Hasdrubal's movements, deploying his own forces in opposition, ready to fight. And yet nothing happened: 'both the armies stood drawn up before their ramparts; and as neither party began the attack, and the sun was now going down, the Carthaginian first, and then the Roman, led back his troops into the camp' (Livy 28.14.2). Hasdrubal had moved off relatively late in the day, perhaps indicating that his deployment was intended more for display than for giving battle, but Scipio matched his inaction. It is possible that Hasdrubal's lack of initiative stemmed from his force actually being closer to Scipio's in size (Livy's 54,500 as opposed to Polybius' 74,000); without distinct dominance in numbers, and with no obvious tactical advantage to be gained from terrain either, it is understandable that Hasdrubal and Scipio both might have balked at launching an attack on such even terms.

The following day the same thing happened; Hasdrubal led his army down onto the plain, followed by Scipio in response, where they both waited in the baking sun until the light began to fail and the Carthaginians withdrew to their camp, followed in turn by the Romans. And yet again the day after: 'Neither party sallied from their posts, nor was a weapon discharged, or a word uttered' (Livy 28.14.3). Both armies had deployed against each other on successive days as if in compliance with a script, with little or no variation as to overall behaviour or the positioning of individual units. It was Hasdrubal's habit to have the centre of his line made up of his Libyo-Phoenicians, with his Iberian allies constituting the army's two wings. The cavalry was split equally and positioned on the edge of either wing, together with the elephants standing like castles (Polybius has them on the wings with the cavalry, Livy studded along the whole battle line), the whole force screened by a skirmish line of light infantry. The Roman dispositions were something of a mirror image: the centre of the line was made up of the two legions and their *alae*, while both wings were held by Iberian allies; the cavalry were evenly divided and positioned at the extreme end of each wing, while the whole force was screened by a skirmish line of *velites*.

Scipio saw an opportunity in this martial theatre. After three days of the same thing, it seemed like a reasonable bet that the Carthaginians would use the same deployment the next day as well. Scipio decided to reverse the

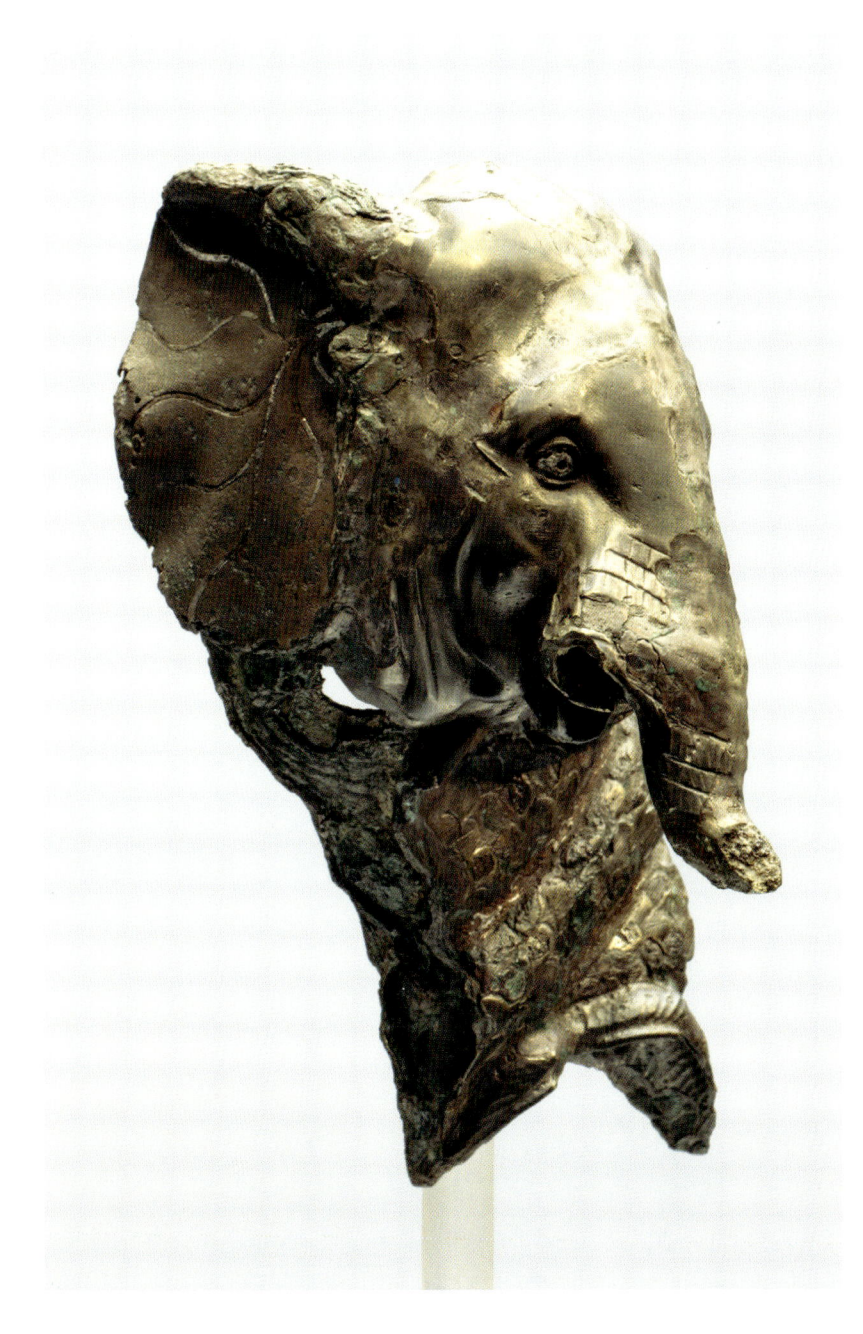

A Roman bust of a war elephant, from the Staatliche Antikensammlungen (State Collection of Antiquities) in Munich, Germany. Information on Hasdrubal Gisco's use of his 32 elephants at Ilipa is frustratingly patchy. The traditional method of employment was to place them in front of the main infantry line, spaced about 30m apart with the intervening gaps filled by light infantry of one type or another (Hoyos 2011: 106), where their very presence could induce panic in an attacker. Livy mentions the elephants at Ilipa, standing in a line at the front of the army in the deployments on the days prior to the battle (Livy 28.14.4), while Polybius says nothing of that, instead noting that on the day of battle Hasdrubal had his elephants on the wings with his cavalry (11.24), something confirmed in Livy who notes that the elephants, distressed by the attacks upon them on the flanks, retreated to the centre of the main Carthaginian line (28.15.5). (MatthiasKabel/Wikimedia/ CC BY-SA 3.0)

disposition of his main line, positioning the Iberians in the centre and his legions on either wing. If Hasdrubal deployed as expected, Scipio would have his strongest troops bearing down on Hasdrubal's Iberians, but to ensure that Hasdrubal played his part Scipio would have to seize the initiative:

> He issued orders through the camp at evening, that the men and horses should be refreshed and fed before daylight, and that the horsemen, armed themselves, should keep their horses bridled and saddled. When it was scarcely yet daylight, he sent all his cavalry, with the light troops, against the Carthaginian outposts, and then without delay advanced himself, at the head of the heavy body of the

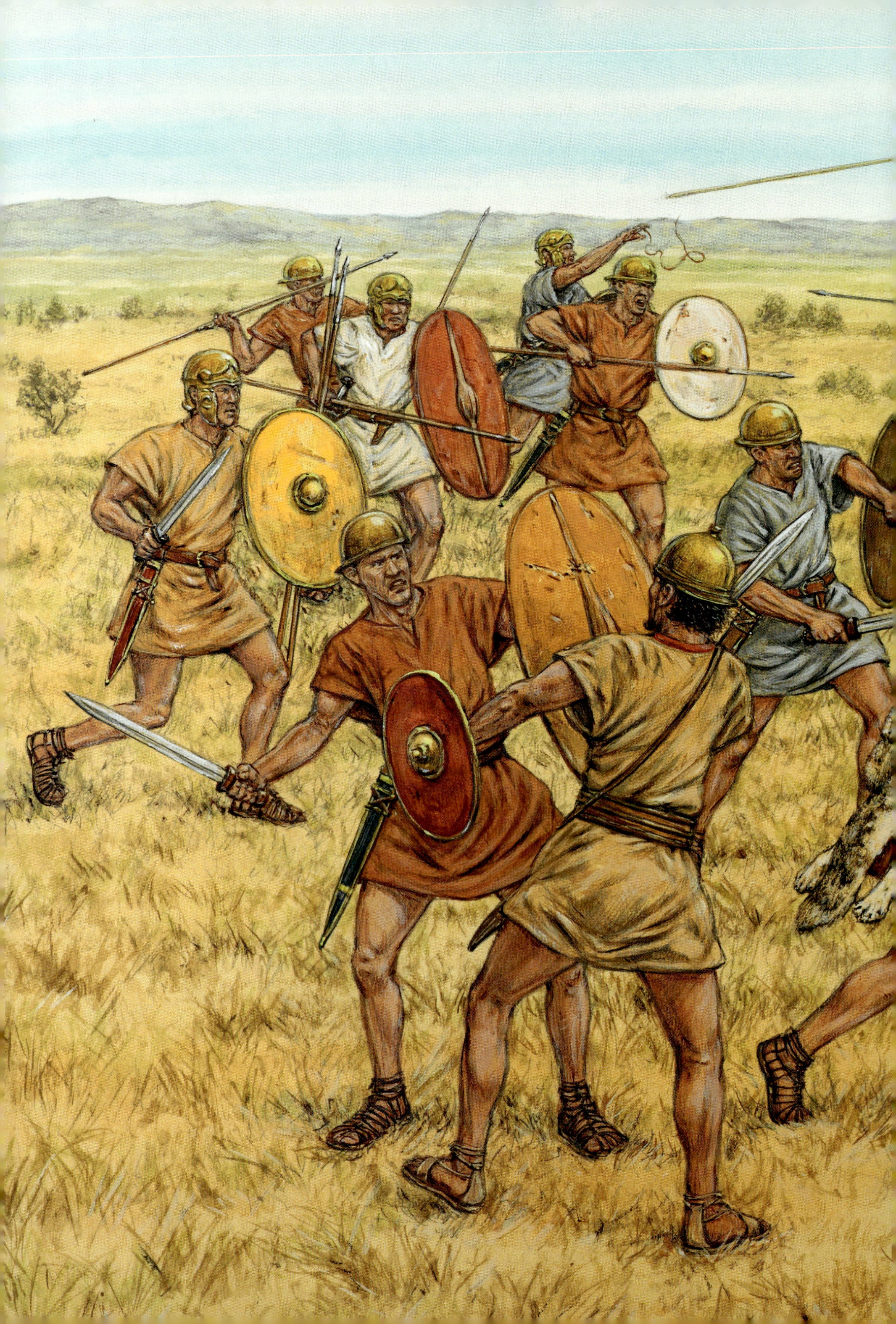

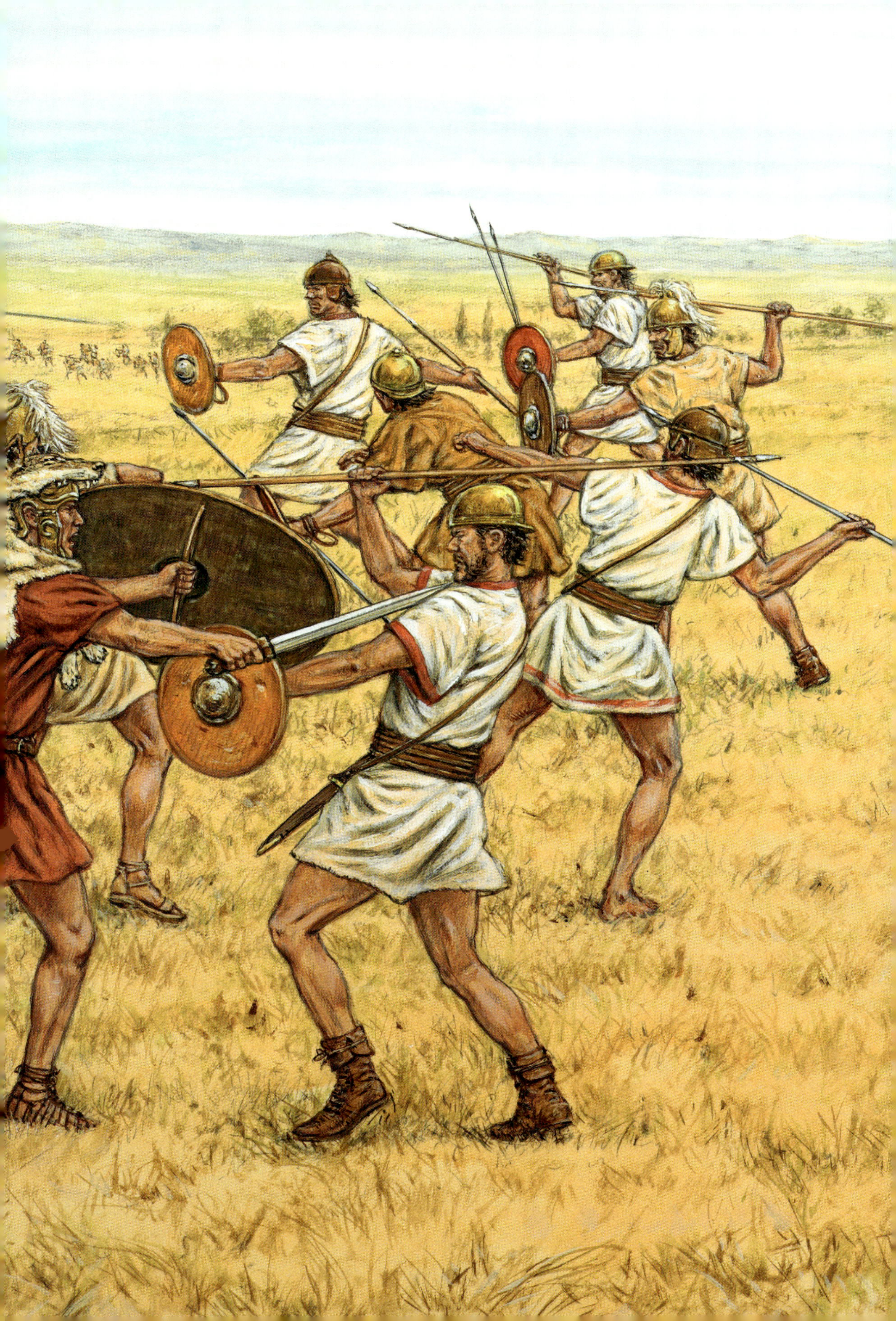

PREVIOUS PAGES

Skirmishing between the lines

The light troops of Roman and Carthaginian armies, like those of later ages, often fought their own private battles well forward of their respective forces, trying to gain the upper hand and thus bring their arrows, spears and sling bullets within range of their foe's main line. On the morning of battle Hasdrubal Gisco's army has rushed to form up opposite Scipio's threatening battle line, while Roman *velites* advance on the Carthaginian force's screen of light infantry; missiles are exchanged as the two bodies of light troops dart back and forth, and as the morning drags on a series of intense localized skirmishes ensue. At one point the Iberians and Romans have come into contact, sparking a number of fast, vicious hand-to-hand combats. Several *velites* are casting their light spears (in one case using a coiled string to impart extra accuracy to his throw), while others dodge away from a hurled Iberian *saunion* (known as the *soliferrum* – literally 'just iron' – to the Romans). Several pairs of combatants are slashing and feinting at one another, while a *veles* with a wolfskin-decorated helmet catches an Iberian spear-thrust with his shield, batting it away and slashing his *gladius* at the throat of his foe.

---

legions, having strengthened his wings with Roman soldiers, and placed the allies in the centre, contrary to the full anticipations of his own men and of the enemy. (Livy 28.14.7–9)

Scipio's gambit had the desired effect. The rapid advance of Roman cavalry and *velites* not long after the sun had broken the horizon landed upon the enemy as a complete surprise; the Carthaginian outposts were overrun and a general sense of alarm spread through the whole camp. Hasdrubal scrambled from his tent, ordering his army to arms at once, dispatching his cavalry and light infantry to keep the Romans at bay while he pulled the rest of his force together to meet this unexpected threat. The Libyo-Phoenicians and Iberians hurried into their arms and, without breakfast, began deploying onto the plain behind a roiling screen of cavalry attack and counter-attack, positioning themselves as they had done each previous day, with Hasdrubal's main strength in the centre once again, his wings manned by his Iberian allies. Once on the field, Hasdrubal must have soon discovered that the Romans had changed the balance of their line, but he was already drawn up for battle and too close to the enemy to be able to make any change to his existing dispositions without exposing himself to immediate attack.

Separate battles between the opposing cavalry and light infantry see-sawed between the two armies for most of the morning, with neither side developing any advantage; if the fight was going against a particular troop or group of light infantry, they quickly retreated towards the safety of their main line, resting for a time before sallying forth once again to resume the attack. Eventually Scipio gave the signal to retreat, whereupon the cavalry and *velites* broke off their attacks and pulled back through the intervals in the maniples in his army's main line, whereupon they distributed themselves into two groups and formed up behind the wings, *velites* in front and cavalry behind. The whole Roman line then began to advance.

Scipio himself was positioned on the right wing of the line, his trusted subordinates Lucius Marcius and Marcus Junius Silanus on the left wing, ensuring that the next manoeuvre would be executed exactly as Scipio wished. Each wing was already in the *triplex acies* pattern when, while still around

A bronze 'Pilos' helmet, Greek, 5th century BC or later, of the sort that would have been worn by various troops within Hannibal's armies. This style of helmet was derived from a common brimless travelling cap of similar shape usually made of felt or leather; it was a simple and effective form of head protection, supposedly first popularized by the Spartans, and it became common among various types of Hellenistic foot soldiers. In comparison to the more florid helmets of the Corinthian or Attic style it was light, cheap and quick to produce, and though it offered less protection to the face and neck it allowed the wearer to see and hear unimpeded. (Metropolitan Museum of Art, www.metmuseum.org)

700m from the enemy, the order was given for them to turn (the right wing to the right, mirrored by the left wing turning to the left), effectively transforming the three lines of each wing into three columns (with a column of *velites* and a column of cavalry as well). The columns advanced outwards left and right before wheeling, still in column, to face the outer edges of the Carthaginian line; resuming their forward advance, their faster pace (columns almost always move faster than lines) meant that they outstripped their own allies in the centre who were still marching forward slowly, line abreast. As they drew close to the Carthaginian wings, both Roman columns wheeled 90 degrees inwards, returning to the *triplex acies* line, while the cavalry and *velites* wheeled in the opposite direction, swinging around either end of the Carthaginian line.

The manoeuvre executed by Scipio's Roman legions has been the source of much historical discussion, some tactical due to the apparently overly complex nature of the movements involved, some linguistic because of difficulties in interpreting Polybius' exact meaning – for his part, Livy does not give a detailed description of the action. (For those wishing to examine Scipio's tactical manoeuvres in greater detail, two of the more interesting modern interpretations are those given by the historians Peter Connolly (1998: 199–201) and John Lazenby (1998: 147–50).) In any event, Scipio's intention was to throw his legions against Hasdrubal's weakest troops on the Carthaginian wings, while his cavalry and light infantry wheeled around the ends of the line to achieve a double-envelopment – and that appears to be exactly what happened. Hasdrubal's best troops, the Libyo-Phoenician heavy infantry in the centre of his line, were not yet engaged as the creeping Roman-allied centre had yet to even come within javelin range, but they could offer no help to the beleaguered Iberians on their left and right as that would expose them to a potentially devastating counter-attack from that slow-moving enemy line in front of them. The Carthaginian cavalry and light infantry seem to have played no part in interfering with the Roman manoeuvres, having been withdrawn to the wings to await the attack, though it is possible that they were positioned in such a manner by Hasdrubal in anticipation of being employed as a counter-attacking or enveloping force against the legions when they were fully engaged with the Iberian wings. Such a tactic would make sense, especially when employing elephants as well, bearing in mind the havoc they tended to cause in organized bodies of troops, but if that was Hasdrubal's intention then it was stymied by Scipio's own use of his light infantry and cavalry, which precluded anything other than a defensive response.

Scipio's simultaneous attack on both wings of Hasdrubal's army brought terrible pressure to bear on the defenders, 'Balearians and raw Spaniards' (Livy 28.15.1), who were fighting hard for their lives against the best that Rome and its Latin allies had to offer. The attacks by the cavalry and the *velites* on the flanks took a particular toll on Hasdrubal's elephants, Polybius describing how 'When these troops were at close quarters the elephants were severely handled, being wounded and harassed on every side by the velites and cavalry, and did as much harm to their friends as to their foes; for they rushed about promiscuously and killed every one that fell in their way on either side alike' (11.24).

The disadvantage of their quick deployment so early in the morning now began to tell on the Carthaginians. They had been forced onto the field with no food and presumably little water other than that which individual soldiers carried with them. They had been standing in the slowly growing heat of the day for hours, resting on their shields as Scipio's cavalry and *velites* engaged in a seemingly interminable back-and-forth struggle with their own light troops and horsemen; their army seemed to have lost all initiative, and now the Romans had both ends of the Carthaginian line trapped in a vice, and were squeezing hard.

The Carthaginian line, battered at every turn, began ever so slowly to give way, ironically it being the Libyo-Phoenicians in the centre who were the first to falter. At the outset the retreat was barely perceptible, being slow and steady, as if under the orders of Hasdrubal himself. His men were gradually giving ground under the constant pressure exerted by the Romans, but 'when the victors, perceiving that the enemy had given way, charged them on all sides with increased vehemence on that very account, so that the shock could hardly be sustained, though Hasdrubal endeavoured to stop them and hinder them from retiring' (Livy 28.15.6–7). What had been a reluctant withdrawal became something closer to a panicked retreat. Even so, their position need not have been calamitous as long as the cohesion of their lines held, for their path of retreat led to the base of the hill on which their camp was sited; but the aggression of the Romans was too much, with 'fear getting the better of their sense of shame, and all those who were nearest the enemy giving way, they immediately turned their backs, and all gave themselves up to disorderly flight' (Livy 28.15.8–9).

The general rout of Hasdrubal's army was stopped all too briefly at the base of the hills where the Carthaginian camp lay, but the consistent pressure applied by the closely following Romans quickly broke their fragile resolve and Hasdrubal's men fled back through their own fortifications into their camp. It is likely that Scipio could have forced matters to a grim conclusion there and then, but a sudden turn in the weather led to a thunderstorm that bogged the Romans down, forcing them to abandon their pursuit and return to their own lines. Through the night Hasdrubal's Iberian allies melted away, and though some small efforts were made to reinforce the camp's defences with local stonework, the loss of his allies decided the matter for Hasdrubal, who chose to withdraw with all dispatch.

Scipio gave chase at first light the next day, with his cavalry and light infantry in the vanguard, harrying the flanks and rear of the broken Carthaginian army at every opportunity. The necessity of fighting off such repeated attacks delayed the retreat, which allowed time for the legions to catch up with the vanguard, whereupon Livy describes the scene as being 'no longer a fight, but a butchering as of cattle' (28.16.6). Hasdrubal managed to flee into the neighbouring hills with a rump of 6,000 men, the rest falling to slavery or the sword. Though the remnants of the Carthaginian army found that they could keep the Romans at bay due to their well-chosen position in the hills, their situation – with half the men unarmed, negligible provisions and no prospect of relief – was insupportable. All too soon the survivors deserted or gave themselves up, with Hasdrubal abandoning his dying army during the night, fleeing back to Gades and making good his escape by sea.

The cohesion of the various bodies of troops that was so crucial a part of Carthaginian command was broken by Scipio's attack, the threads that bound the various elements of Hasdrubal's army together dissolving in the thunderstorm that followed. Once that sense of control had been lost, it was impossible for Hasdrubal to succeed against Scipio, the disintegration of his army becoming an inevitability under continuous Roman pressure. There are no figures for casualties at Ilipa, though the turn in the weather surely stopped the Carthaginian losses from being too great on the day of battle. In most defeats, however, the real damage tends to be done during the losing side's retreat, and such certainly seems to have been the case for Hasdrubal's unfortunate force.

A bronze helmet with cheek-guards, Etruscan, from the mid-4th century BC. It is of the 'jockey-cap' type with a hemispherical crown topped with a knob often decorated with a rosette. The cheek-guards are hinged and decorated with a 'triple-disc' pattern that was a popular style among Celts (it probably had its origins in the Celtic tribes from southern Germany), but which was also worn by Iberian and no doubt some Roman troops as well; examples of breastplates following a similar design also exist. (Metropolitan Museum of Art, www.metmuseum.org)

Analysis

LAKE TRASIMENE

Like Cannae that followed it, Trasimene is seen as an exercise in military brilliance. Hannibal set out to gain the strategic initiative from Flaminius, and once he achieved it he never lost it, seemingly drawing the Roman army whichever way he pleased. Trasimene also offers one of the key lessons of generalship in the classical world, namely that Hannibal had completed all his preparations long before the two sides ever met; when the time came all he had to do was issue a single, simple order to put his plan into effect, all his subordinates and their men knowing what they were supposed to do. As for his ambush, whether long-planned or the genesis of a set of circumstances that he found before him, it was a reasonable gamble that paid a spectacular dividend, though it is worth remembering that victories like Trasimene are only as complete and devastating as they are because the enemy 'plays his part' by doing all the wrong things at all the wrong times. Few commanders are lucky enough to have such an opponent.

The Romans made some notable errors in the immediate prelude to the battle, the most significant of which was their failure to throw forward any sort of reconnaissance force to probe the potentially devastating area of ground into which the whole Roman army was about to march. Flaminius' aggressive pursuit of Hannibal was hardly an unusual act, especially considering the damage that Hannibal was inflicting upon the lands and properties of Rome's Italian allies, but the way in which he executed that pursuit does seem to have been unusually careless. Hannibal's force outstripped that of Flaminius by many thousands, added to which he had already proved that he could fight and win against a Roman army on far closer odds. It is possible that there were reasons for Flaminius' behaviour that are not understood because we simply do not have enough information on the matter – the chance that he was acting in closer concert with Servilius than we realize, for example.

Even so, the rashness of his close pursuit of an extremely strong enemy into unknown terrain without any sort of screen bespeaks a mixture of arrogance and thoughtlessness that would prove fatal for many more men than Flaminius himself.

The ambush was the perfect opportunity for Hannibal's Gauls, light horsemen and other irregulars to make the most of their varied fighting styles. Gaulish charges, while they could be terrifyingly intimidating, rarely succeeded against a well-disciplined line of legionaries who were prepared to receive them, but that was not the case at Trasimene. The Gauls fell on the long unguarded flank of a column, the surprise, speed and ferocity of their first attack wrecking any chance that the legions may have had to put up a proper battle line. The lack of space to manoeuvre meant that it was not possible for the legionaries to disengage and re-form, thus forcing them to fight on their enemy's terms. The short-term success of the vanguard was impressive in the circumstances, but the small victory they gained could not be used to the Roman army's – or their – advantage, so quick was the immolation of the rest of the force, so strong the immediate pursuit that was launched to bring them to heel.

CANNAE

The actions of Quintus Fabius Maximus prior to Cannae proved effective despite their unpopularity, though it was unlikely that a strategy based on delay and evasion would ever bring a decisive victory over the Carthaginian armies in Italia. Sooner or later Hannibal would have to be brought to heel and destroyed; his army's capability to roam where it pleased, living off the land, was an intolerable state of affairs for the government of Rome, as Hannibal well knew, so a clash was inevitable. The Roman decision to try to draw Hannibal into a battle was not necessarily bad; they outnumbered him, and any halfway-serious defeat for the Carthaginians would probably mean the disintegration of their army and the end of the Punic menace, at least on the mainland.

Hannibal clearly understood the mind-set of his enemies, which appeared to be one of straightforward aggression unchanged from Trasimene. The seemingly infinite Roman proclivity for intemperate action reasserted itself in disastrous form once again, and yet again it was a case of the Romans allowing Hannibal to dictate when, where and how he would fight. The observations of Polybius on the importance of cavalry – 'in actual war it is better to have half the number of infantry, and the superiority in cavalry, than to engage your enemy with an equality in both' (3.117) – are borne out by the events at Cannae, but only in as much as the Romans opted to fight on good ground for horses even though their opponents outnumbered them by very nearly 2 to 1 in cavalry. Varro and Paullus took no other action to try to mitigate the threat that Hannibal's horsemen posed either to Rome's horsemen or to its infantry.

The haste with which the legions were raised and pressed into service, exacerbating the issues inherent in a lack of training, may also have been a factor. The decision to compress the Roman line, thus hampering one of the

The remains of a Roman spearhead. Polybius noted how 'it is a peculiarity of the Roman people as a whole to treat everything as a question of main strength; to consider that they must of course accomplish whatever they have proposed to themselves; and that nothing is impossible that they have once determined upon. The result of such self-confidence is that in many things they do succeed, while in some few they conspicuously fail, and especially at sea' (1.37). Aggressiveness was an important quality in Roman warfare and also in Roman society, a situation in which both spheres probably fed off one another, often resulting in glory but also on occasion, as the early battles of the Second Punic War such as Trasimene tended to show, in disastrous reverses. (Science & Society Picture Library/Getty Images)

legion's major advantages – manipular tactics – was also unusual, though it may have been in response to the callowness of many of the troops engaged, who would probably have lacked the experience to execute such manoeuvres properly, making a more traditional deployment a simpler option. As for leadership, Paullus is cast as the hero, Varro the villain, but the split leadership was the most serious of the problems they faced, making it impossible to have any consistent plan or even approach to deal with the threat posed by Hannibal. Varro, being the commander on the day, must take the lion's share of responsibility for such carelessness in the face of an opponent of known skill and experience, though somewhat like Flaminius at Trasimene Varro did seem to make decisions that accorded very much with his enemy's wishes. Rome would have to learn how to win against Hannibal's military system, a process that would necessitate ever-greater efforts in the raising and especially the training of new legions to replace those immolated at Cannae, as well as the promotion of new commanders such as Scipio, a man with much to prove, and avenge.

ILIPA

Ilipa is often touted as the apotheosis of Scipio's tactical genius, the deployment of his army to effect a 'reverse Cannae' being seen as worthy of Hannibal himself. Leaving aside such hyperbole, his victory is noteworthy not just for its strategic implications (which were significant), but for its demonstration of Scipio as a man who had learned to take advantage of his enemy's failings. Scipio's decision to reverse his deployment was not the culmination of some long-nurtured strategy; it came about as a direct result of the circumstances in which he found himself, facing an opponent of (probably) greater strength, whose behaviour was predictable and therefore exploitable. It is to Scipio's credit that he made the most of the opportunity, though it is interesting to wonder what might have happened if Hasdrubal had been more aggressive on the preceding days, forcing Scipio into a more straightforward fight.

Though it is difficult to understand the exact nature of Scipio's complex pattern of manoeuvres that led to the double-envelopment at Ilipa, it is possible to say that they seem to have been carried out flawlessly, which is a good indication of the high degree of training that the Roman (and, one assumes, to a lesser extent, the allied) legions had undergone while under Scipio's command – such a high degree of professionalism was not on display in the war's earlier years. The execution of such a tactical realignment would require well-drilled troops who had the discipline and nerve to perform it in the face of the enemy; it also shows Scipio to have planned out his battle with great care, and the necessary trust he must have placed in his subordinates to carry out his orders as he had given them.

In comparison, Hasdrubal Gisco does not emerge with much glory. He had won a notable victory at the Upper Baetis in 211 BC (the only major Carthaginian victory not to come at Hannibal's hands), and his initial moves towards Ilipa bespoke an aggressive man in search of a fight. Nevertheless his late-in-the-day deployments hint at a degree of indecision, or a desire to let his enemy make the running for him by starting the battle, something

Epigraph for Scipio after his victory in the Second Punic War, from the collections of the Museo Della Civiltà Romana. (De Agostini Picture Library/Getty Images)

Scipio did do, though not in the way Hasdrubal anticipated. Once the battle developed, Hasdrubal seemed unable to respond to the Roman attack; he lost the initiative with Scipio's early morning deployment, and he never came close to getting it back, instead apparently waiting to receive whatever the Romans decided to deliver. His decision to break camp seems to be of a part with his earlier failure, however understandable it might be in the light of the desertion of his allies.

The Carthaginian loss at Ilipa had significant strategic consequences. By securing Iberia Scipio cut off one of Hannibal's most valuable sources of money and manpower, effectively hamstringing any further Carthaginian attempts to reinforce Hannibal's position in Italia with another invasion force. With little prospect of effective reinforcement and no chance of victory without it, Hannibal would be recalled from Latin lands, while the initiative for the final phase of the war passed to an ascendant Roman state, set on vengeance.

Aftermath

Rome's early defeats were increasingly severe, with the engagements at Ticinus, the Trebia and particularly Lake Trasimene proving to be profoundly humiliating as well as strategically serious. The remedy – to crush Hannibal with an overwhelming hammer-blow of military might – backfired spectacularly, resulting in a defeat of such epic proportions that it is still a common subject of discussion among students of history and warfare over 22 centuries later.

Those early drubbings delivered by Hannibal necessitated some change in the Roman military system, though not in any of its essential characteristics. There was a massive expansion of the legions and their associated *alae* in the succeeding years to meet the needs of a war fought in Italia, Sicilia and Iberia at the same time, growth that was augmented by better training of the legionaries; Scipio's manoeuvres at Ilipa would not have been possible unless his army was extremely well-drilled and a much more disciplined force than that which took the field at Cannae. The Roman armies that would go on to dominate the Hellenistic world throughout the following century were effectively forged in the fires of the Hannibalic wars.

For the Carthaginians, the great promise of Hannibal's early successes seemed to stall and dwindle into years of fruitless manoeuvrings that never managed to bring Rome as close to defeat as it had been in the wake of the catastrophe at Cannae. Hannibal's strategy of splintering the close-knit shield-wall of alliances that surrounded Rome had some limited success, but never enough to drive the city to seek terms with him. Battle casualties and wastage saw the character of the Carthaginian army evolve over the years, with more Gauls, Italians and Iberians and fewer Africans in the ranks, though such changes were not disruptive in a military structure that was predicated on using troops and allies 'as they came'.

Juvenal saw Hannibal as an archetype of vaulting military ambition: 'Nought is accomplished until my Punic host breaks down the city gates, and

FAR LEFT
The suicide of Dido, Queen of Carthage, by Ferdinando Tacca (1619–86), c.1630–50. In abandoning his lover Dido, Aeneas of Troy – the mythic founder of Rome – is displaying *pietas* (a sense of personal duty and responsibility that one owes to one's family and one's people) in deferring to his destiny, but in so doing he destroys Dido and earns the lasting enmity of her people. Even when Virgil was composing the *Aeneid*, well over 100 years after the final destruction of Carthage, the cultural memory of the rivalry between the two states was still important enough to see it woven into the fabric of Roman foundational storytelling. (Metropolitan Museum of Art, www.metmuseum.org)

LEFT
A statue of Hannibal counting the rings of Roman *equites* killed at Cannae, by Sébastien Slodtz (1655–1726), 1704. Barely past 30 years of age, Hannibal had inflicted the most severe defeat on Rome in centuries. The unfortunate reality for Hannibal, however, was that his greatest military triumph – the latest in a series of impressive and increasingly significant victories – would get him no closer to his goal, the subjugation of Rome. For the next ten years he would campaign throughout Italia, but strategic victory would always remain outside his grasp. (VCG Wilson/Corbis via Getty Images)

I plant my standard in the midst of the Subura! [one of Rome's less salubrious neighbourhoods]' (*Satires* 10.154–56). Ironically, it would be the lack of just such an ambition that kept victory out of his grasp. Hannibal understood Roman drive and aggression on the battlefield, using it for his own ends, but he failed to appreciate that such an attitude was not merely a feature of the Roman legions but was one of the defining characteristics of the state he was trying to subdue. The very fact that he thought Roman Italia could be brought to heel without destroying the heart of the problem – the city of Rome itself – is testament to this. However brilliant his tactical endeavours, his strategic vision was fundamentally flawed, leaving the way open for more flexible and capable men such as Scipio to rise up and meet him on their terms, not his.

Scipio's victory in Iberia was strategically disastrous for the Carthaginians, resulting in the effective containment of the diminished Carthaginian armies on the Italian mainland and allowing Scipio to prosecute an invasion of North Africa that was so successful it necessitated Hannibal's recall, the two great generals finally meeting at Zama in 202 BC. The army that was fielded by Hannibal and the Carthaginians had a core of veterans at its heart but it was nowhere near as cohesive or well-trained as the Roman force that opposed it, and thus was soundly beaten. That defeat effectively finished Carthage as a state with anything more than local influence, and it never again escaped Rome's shadow, finally receiving the *coup de grâce* at the climax of the Third Punic War in 146 BC, surrounded and destroyed once and for all by its most unforgiving and merciless enemy.

BIBLIOGRAPHY

Ancient sources

Appian (c.AD 95–c.165) was born in Alexandria but moved to Rome in his adulthood. Written in Greek, his *Roman History* gives a sequential account of Rome's conquests, all the way up to the early 2nd century AD. His work drew on many earlier sources, including Polybius, some of which are lost. His history comes from a decidedly Roman perspective, explaining the Empire's growth and military success through qualities such as endurance, patience and virtue (Hornblower & Spawforth 1996: 130).

Ennius (239–169 BC) was famous in his own time and for centuries afterwards for his *Annales*, a poetical history of Rome from the fall of Troy to his present age. Despite their widespread popularity his works are almost completely lost. His value comes from the fact that he lived through the Second Punic War, and his opinions on the conflict (scant though they are) may well reflect those of his contemporary society.

Juvenal was a Roman poet active around the end of the 1st century AD, famous for his 16 biting and full-throated *Satires* on Roman life and society.

Titus Livius (usually known as **Livy**, 64 or 59 BC–AD 12 or 17) undertook the monumental task of writing the entire history of Rome, from the city's founding in 753 BC to his own time, in 142 volumes, 35 of which still exist more or less intact. He drew on a number of disparate sources for his work on the Second Punic War, with Polybius being essential, but he also used the writings of men such as Valerius Antias (a Roman annalist of the 1st century BC whose works are now lost) and Quintus Fabius Pictor (a veteran of the Second Punic War who wrote a history, also now lost) to provide him with much of his information regarding the campaigns in Italia after Trasimene. Despite his reliance on earlier authors, Livy was not simply a copyist; for example, he makes a point of criticizing what he sees as Valerius' exaggerated statistics for Roman/Carthaginian battle casualties (Erdkamp 2006). Some of his accounts of military life and campaigns are of great value, but unlike Polybius Livy was not a soldier and thus his interpretations can be suspect. Nevertheless he represents probably the most important source for information on the Carthaginian wars after Polybius.

The treatise on generalship written by **Onasander**, the *Strategikos*, was composed some time in the middle of the 1st century AD. Onasander saw his military work as a practical guide to good generalship, emphasizing the strong moral and intellectual requirements that such positions demanded of those who would fill them.

The *Histories* of **Polybius** (c. 200–c. 118 BC) covered the rise of Roman power from 264 BC down to the Third Punic War (149–146 BC) in 40 books, the first five of which have survived in their entirety, the remainder in fragments of varying sizes. A Greek soldier and aristocrat, he was shipped to Rome as a political detainee in 167 BC and found a place in Roman high society. Much of the value in his works, written in Greek, comes from the fact that he was aiming to explain to 'foreigners' (his erstwhile countrymen) what it was that made Rome and its armies so successful. He also had a first-hand view of the Roman army at work (including the sack of Carthage in 146 BC), and drew on a wide range of sources that included not only pre-existing histories and accounts, but also on conversations with surviving eyewitnesses such as Hannibal's Numidian cavalry commander Masinissa (Hoyos 2015: 283). Polybius was able to understand such men as he was the son of a general and had also been a cavalry commander, giving him a thorough grounding in the theory and practice of warfare. Dexter Hoyos observed that when Polybius' account of a battle or campaign diverges from that of writers such as Livy or Appian, it is his version that usually proves to be the more reliable (Hoyos 2015: 283).

Silius Italicus (c.AD 26–102), a noted politician and poet, composed the 17-book *Punica*, an epic poem that took as its subject the Second Punic War. Blending history drawn from Livy with the poetics of the *Aeneid*, Silius' work is useful in demonstrating Rome's historical view of itself, and for casting Hannibal as the personification of divine wrath.

Cassius Dio (c.AD 164–after 229) was a distinguished Greek senator and author of an 80-volume history of Rome, from the city's founding until AD 229. Some parts are fully extant, but much of the work is lost; an intermittently valuable abridgement of his text by the Byzantine historian Johannes Zonaras helps to fill some of the gaps. Written in Attic Greek, Dio's *Roman History* is something of a Graeco-Roman hybrid, and while most of the sources he used in composing his work are uncertain, his interpretations seem to be of his own making rather than rote repetitions of other men's views. He could be slapdash and error-prone, and also had a proclivity for supernatural events, paying much attention to portents and their interpretations (Hornblower & Spawforth 1996: 299–300).

Classical works

Cassius Dio, trans. Ernest Cary (1914). *Dio's Roman History*. Loeb Classical Library 175. London: William Heinemann.

Ennius, trans. E.H. Warmington (1935). *Remains of Old Latin I: Ennius and Caecilius*. Loeb Classical Library 294. Cambridge, MA: Harvard University Press.

Juvenal, trans. G.G. Ramsay (1928). *Juvenal and Persius*. Loeb Classical Library 91. London: William Heinemann.

Onasander, trans. Illinois Greek Club (1923). *Aeneas Tacticus, Asclepiodotus, and Onasander*. Loeb Classical Library 156. Cambridge, MA: Harvard University Press.

Livy, trans. Cyrus Edmonds (1850). *The History of Rome. Books Twenty-Seven to Thirty-Six.* London: Henry G. Bohn.
Livy, trans. Cyrus Edmonds (1922). *The History of Rome by Titus Livius. Books XXI and XXII.* New York, NY: Translation Publishing Company.
Polybius, trans. Evelyn S. Shuckburgh (1889). *The Histories of Polybius* (two volumes). London: Macmillan.
Silius Italicus, trans. J.D. Duff (1927). *Punica.* Loeb Classical Library 277. London: William Heinemann.

Modern works

Beard, Mary (2016). *SPQR: A History of Ancient Rome.* London: Profile Books.
Bishop, M.C. (2016). *The Gladius: The Roman Short Sword.* Weapon 51. Oxford: Osprey.
Bishop, M.C. (2017). *The Pilum: The Roman Heavy Javelin.* Weapon 55. Oxford: Osprey.
Bishop, M.C. & Coulston, J.C.N. (2006). *Roman Military Equipment: From the Punic Wars to the Fall of Rome (2nd Edition).* Oxford: Oxbow Books.
Brunt, P.A. (2001). *Italian Manpower 225 B.C.–A.D. 14.* Oxford: Oxford University Press. First published in 1971.
Burns, Michael T. (2003). 'The Homogenisation of Military Equipment under the Roman Republic', in *Digressus*, supplement 1 (2003): 60–85.
Connolly, Peter (1998). *Greece and Rome at War.* London: Greenhill.
Daly, Gregory (2002). *Cannae: The Experience of Battle in the Second Punic War.* London: Routledge.
Erdkamp, Paul (2006). 'Late-Annalistic Battle Scenes in Livy (Books 21–44)', in *Mnemosyne*, Fourth Series, Vol. 59, Fasc. 4: 525–63.
Erdkamp, Paul, ed. (2007). *A Companion to the Roman Army.* Oxford: Blackwell Publishing.
Fields, Nic (2007). *The Roman Army of the Punic Wars 264–146 BC.* Battle Orders 27. Oxford: Osprey.
Fields, Nic (2010). *Carthaginian Warrior 264–146 BC.* Warrior 150. Oxford: Osprey.
Fields, Nic (2017). *Lake Trasimene 217 BC: Ambush and annihilation of a Roman army.* Campaign 303. Oxford: Osprey.
Gilliver, Kate (2007). 'Display in Roman Warfare: The Appearance of Armies and Individuals on the Battlefield', in *War in History* 14.1: 1–21.
Goldsworthy, Adrian (2006). *The Fall of Carthage: The Punic Wars 265–146 BC.* London: Weidenfeld & Nicolson.
Harris, William V. (2016). *Roman Power. A Thousand Years of Empire.* Cambridge: Cambridge University Press.
Healy, Mark (1994). *Cannae 216 BC: Hannibal smashes Rome's Army.* Campaign 36. London: Osprey.
Hornblower, Simon & Spawforth, Antony, eds (1996). *The Oxford Classical Dictionary (3rd Edition).* New York, NY: Oxford University Press.
Hoyos, Dexter (2011). *A Companion to the Punic Wars.* Chichester: Wiley-Blackwell.
Kelly, Amanda (2012). 'The Cretan Slinger at War – A Weighty Exchange', in *The Annual of the British School at Athens*, Vol. 107: 273–311.
Keppie, Lawrence J.F. (1984). *The Making of the Roman Army: From Republic to Empire.* London: Batsford.
Lancel, Serge, trans. Antonia Nevill (1999). *Hannibal.* Oxford: Wiley-Blackwell. Originally published in French in 1995.
Lazenby, John Francis (1998). *Hannibal's War: A Military History of the Second Punic War.* Norman, OK: University of Oklahoma Press.
Lazenby, John Francis (2014). 'Rome and Carthage', in H.I. Flower, ed. *The Cambridge Companion to the Roman Republic*, Cambridge: Cambridge University Press, pp. 260–76.
McDonnell, Myles A. (2006). *Roman Manliness: Virtus and the Roman Republic.* Cambridge: Cambridge University Press.
O'Connell, Kevin P. (2016). *The Battle-site of Ilipa: Back to Basics.* Self-published. Available online at: https://www.academia.edu/24671515/THE_BATTLE-SITE_OF_ILIPA_BACK_TO_BASICS
Rawlings, Louis (1996). 'Celts, Spaniards, and Samnites: Warriors in a Soldiers' War', in Tim Cornell, Boris Rankov & Philip Sabin, eds, *The Second Punic War: A Reappraisal*. London: University of London, Institute of Classical Studies. BICS Supplement 67, pp. 81–95.
Rich, John (1996). 'The Origins of the Second Punic War', in Tim Cornell, Boris Rankov & Philip Sabin, eds, *The Second Punic War: A Reappraisal*. London: University of London, Institute of Classical Studies. BICS Supplement 67, pp. 1–37.
Rosenstein, Nathan S. & Morstein-Marx, Robert, eds (2010). *A Companion to the Roman Republic.* Oxford: Blackwell.
Sabin, Philip (1996). 'The Mechanics of Battle in the Second Punic War', in Tim Cornell, Boris Rankov & Philip Sabin, eds, *The Second Punic War: A Reappraisal*. London: University of London, Institute of Classical Studies. BICS Supplement 67, pp. 59–79.
Sabin, Philip (2000). 'The Face of Roman Battle', in *Journal of Roman Studies* 90: 1–17.
Sabin, Philip, van Wees, Hans & Whitby, Michael, eds (2007). *The Cambridge History of Greek and Roman Warfare, Volume 1: Greece, The Hellenistic World and the Rise of Rome.* Cambridge: Cambridge University Press.
Salimbeti, Andrea & D'Amato, Raffaele (2014). *The Carthaginians 6th–2nd Century BC.* Elite 201. Oxford: Osprey.
Scullard, H.H. (1930). *Scipio Africanus in the Second Punic War.* Cambridge: Cambridge University Press.
Scullard, H.H. (1936). 'A Note on the Battle of Ilipa', in *The Journal of Roman Studies*, Vol. 26, Part 1 (1936): 19–23. Available online at: http://www.jstor.org/stable/296701
Walbank (2007). 'Fortune (*tychē*) in Polybius', in John Marincola, ed. *A Companion to Greek and Roman Historiography*. Oxford: Blackwell, pp. 349–355.
Wise, Terence (1982). *Armies of the Carthaginian Wars 265–146 BC.* Men-at-Arms 121. London: Osprey.

INDEX

References to illustrations are shown in **bold**.

alae (allied legions) 9, 12, 23, 26, 35, 76
  composition/strength 27, 34, 40
  raising/training of 25, 41, 44, 74
  use in combat 34, 37, 40, 48, 49, 50, **52–53**, 54, 56, **61**, 62, 64
  ala dextra/ala sinistra **33**, 35, 39
  cavalry 22, 37, 44, 46, **47**, 48, 49, 51, 55
armour/clothing 4, 19, 21, **42**, 62: cuirasses 19, 21, 22, 23, 42, 43, 49; greaves 10, 15, 17, 19, **49**; linothorax 19, **42**, 49; mail coats/shirts 5, **14**, 21, 23, 40, 49, **52–53**, 54, 57: *lorica hamata* **10**, **12**, 17, 19, 22, 49; *paludamentum* 26–27; pectorals 17, 20; pteruges **42**, 43; *subarmalis* **10**, **14**; tunics **14**, 15, 16

Baecula, battle of (208 BC) 58, 59, 62
Balearian slingers 13, 20, 21, 28, 43
  slingshot/slings 18, 20, **20**, 21, 36, 55, 68
  use in combat 34, 35, 36, 48, 49, 50, 62, 70
belts 11, **14**, **16**, 17, 30, **30**, **31**

Cannae, battle of (216 BC) 9, 37, 41–46, **46**, 58
  Carthaginian forces 13, 19, 23, 28, 42–43, 45, **47**, 48, 49
  dispositions of forces 13, **47**, 49–50, 51
  nature of combat 50–51, **52–53**, 54, 55–56, 73–74, 77
  Roman forces 21, 25, 43–45, 48, 49, 51, 73–74, 77
  significance/overview of 56, 73–74
Carthaginian army
  battle formations 28, **33**, **47**, **61**, 64
  cavalry 21, 22–23, 28, **28**, **33**, 34, 37, 43, 48, **52–53**, 54, 55, **61**, 62, 64, 65, 68, 70
  composition/elements of 12, 13, 16, 19–20, 21, 22–23, 25, 28, **28**, 29, 34, 35, 37, 42–43, 48, 62, 64, 76
  light infantry **33**, 49, **61**, 65, **66–67**
  reasons for service 25–26
  troop types/tactical styles 13, 16, 28, 73
Carthaginian empire 4, 12–13, 19, 58, 62, 77
Celtiberians/Celto-Iberians 13, 21, 28
Celtic tribes/troops 20, 28, **52–53**, 54, 71
centurions 17, 18, 25, 26, 27, 36, **52–53**, 54
consuls 26, 36, 41, 45, 55, 56, 62

daggers 15, 20, 57: *pugio* **11**, 57

elephants, use of 5, **5**, 28, 60, **61**, 62, 64, 65, **65**, 70
equites 21, 22, **24**, 50, 56, 77
extraordinarii 15, **33**, 35, 36, 39, 40

First Punic War (264–241 BC) 4, 5, 6, 12, 17, 21, 58

Gaius Flaminius Nepos 29, 30, 36
  actions at Lake Trasimene 30–31, 32, **33**, 34, 35, 36, 37–38, 72–73, 74
Gaius Terentius Varro 41, 43, 45
  at Cannae 21, **47**, 48, 49, 51, 56, 73, 74
Gaulish clans/tribes/warriors 4–5, 13, 21, 23, 25, 28, 29, 34, 36, 40, 42–43, 76
  cavalry 23, 28, 46, **47**, 48, 49, 50, 51, 55, 73
  heavy infantry 23, **33**, 36, 38, 46, **47**, 48, 49–50, 51
Gnaeus Servilius Geminus 29, 30, 31, 34, 37, 41, 43, 49, 55, 56, 72

Hamilcar Barca 6, 58, 77
Hannibal Barca 4, 5
  as battlefield tactician 13, 27–28, 34, 72
  at Lake Trasimene **33**, 34, 35–36, 72
  at Cannae 13, **47**, 48–49, 56
  building of army 25
  charisma of 6, 26
  crossing of Alps/Apennines 13, 30
  flawed strategic vision 31, 77
  military ambition of 76–77
  resources from Iberia 6, 19–20, 58, 59, 62
  threat to Rome 6, 25, 29, 31, 40, 56
Hanno 48, 49
Hasdrubal 49
  actions at Cannae 46, **47**, 51, 55, 56
Hasdrubal Barca 28, 58, 59
Hasdrubal Gisco 28, 58, 59, 62
  actions at Ilipa 59, 60, **61**, 64, 65, 68, 69, 70, 71, 74–75
hastati 11, 16–17, 18, 19, 27, **27**, 45
  use in combat 34, 48, **52–53**, 54
helmets **10**, **14**, **16**, 17, 19, 20, 21, 23, **38**, **39**, **39**, 40, **66–67**, **69**, **71**

Iberia
  Carthaginian control in 6, 12, 19, 58
  reinforcements/resupply from 13, 19–20, 21, 58, 59, 62, 75
Iberian allies/levies
  Carthaginian service **33**, 34, 35, 36, 50, **52–53**, 54, 62, 64, 68, 70, 71, 76
  caetrati 20, 28, 34, 50, 60, **61**, 62, **66–67**, 70
  cavalry 21, 23, 28, 35, 36, 43, 46, **47**, 48, 49, 50, 51, 55
  heavy infantry 30, 39, 43, 46, **47**, 48, 50, 51, 62
  scutarii **14**, 15, 20, 28, 34, 49–50, 62
  Roman service 58, 60, **61**, 62, 64, 65, 68
Ilipa, battle of (206 BC) 57–60, **60**
  dispositions of forces 60, **61**, 62, 65, 68–70
  Scipio's tactics 64–65, 68–69, 74, 75
  nature of combat 62, 64, **66–67**, 68–71
  overview/significance of 74–75, 77
Insubrian horsemen 37, 38

javelins 20, 23, 34, 36, 45, 55, 70: *hasta velitaris* **15**; *pilum* **10**, **16**, **18**, 19, 44, 45, 59; *saunion* 62, **66–67**; *soliferrum* 62

Lake Trasimene, battle of (217 BC) 9, 32, **32**, 34, 35, 49, 54, 58
  Carthaginian army **10**, **11**, 31, 32, 34, 40
  dispositions of forces 32, **33**, 73
  Flaminius' failings 32, 36, 72–73, 74
  Hannibal's ambush 26, 32, 34–35, 35–36
  nature of combat 32, 36–37, 37–40, 73
  overview/significance of 40, 41, 72–73, 76
  Roman army **14**, 15, 34
Libyo-Phoenician heavy infantry 13, 19, 43
  arms/armour 19, 40, **52–53**, 54
  use in combat 28, **33**, 34, 35, 36, 39, 46, **47**, 48, 49, 51, **52–53**, 54, 55, **61**, 62, 64, 68, 69, 70
Lucius Aemilius Paullus 41, 45
  actions at Cannae 21, 43, **47**, 48, 49, 51, 55, 56, 73, 74

Mago Barca 28, 49, 58, 59, 62
Maharbal 28, 34, 37, 40, 48, 56
Marcus Atilius Regulus 41, 43, 56
Marcus Minucius Rufus 41, 49
Masinissa 28, 62, **62**, 64
Metaurus, battle of the (207 BC) 58, 59

Numidian cavalry 21, 22–23, **23**, 28, 43
  use in combat 23, **33**, 34, 35, 36, 40, 46, **47**, 48, 49, 51, 55, 56, 62, 64

optiones 18, 21, 26

principes **10**, **11**, 17, 19, 45
  position in battle line 16, 17, 18, 27, **27**
  use in combat 34, 48, **52–53**, 54
Publius Cornelius Scipio Africanus 5, **5**, 58, **63**, 74, **75**
  battle experience/planning 58, 74
  calibre as commander 27, 58, 74
  Iberian command 58, 59, 62
  actions at Ilipa 60, **61**, 62, 64–65, 68–70, 71, 74, 75, 76, 77

Roman army 8–9, 18–19, 64
  age/property qualifications 8, 44
  columns 35–36, 37, 38, 40
  contubernium 25, 38
  development and training of 8–9, 12
  as expression of martial culture 8, 26
  maniples/manipular tactics 18–19, 25, 26, **27**, 49, 51, **52–53**, 54, 68, 74
  quincunx pattern 18
  supplementa system 9
  triplex acies 16–17, 18, **27**, 38, 68–69
Roman cavalry 16, 17, 21, 23, 26, 48
  battle formations 21, **33**, 35, **47**, 59, **61**
  command/composition of *turmae* 21, 26
  position in legion 27
  selection for 22
  training of 21–22, 44–45
  use in combat 21, 34, 37, 46, **47**, 48, 49, 51, 55, 56, 60, **61**, 62, 64, 68, 69–70, 71
Roman legionaries 11, 17, **18**, **24**, 35
  and military glory 24
  position in battle formations 50, **52–53**, 54, 59
  training of 8, 76
  use in combat 36, 37, 38, 51, 55–56, 59, 64
Roman legions 9, 12, 26
  battle formations **27**, **33**, **47**, **61**
  cavalry element 21, 22, **27**, **33**, 34, **47**, **61**
  citizenry service in 24–25
  composition/strength of 16–17, 21, 22, **27**, 34, 48
  legio I **33**, 34, 35
  legio III **33**, 34, 35, 37
  raising/expansion of 9, 41, 44, 73, 76
  training of 44, 73, 74, 76
  use in combat 25, 32, 34, 46, **47**, 48, 51, 56, 60, **61**, 62, 64, 65, **66–67**, 68–69, 71, 73
  position in battle formations 50, **52–53**, 54, 64, 65, 68–69
  organization of 16–17, **27**

Saguntum, siege of (219 BC) 6, 37, 57
shields 9, **10**, **14**, **16**, 17, 19, 20, 21, 22, 23, 35, 39, 50, 59, 62, **66–67**
spearheads 44, 73
spears 20, 21, 22, 23, 28, 40, 62, **66–67**, 68: *hasta* 17; *sarissa* 19, **52–53**, 54
swords 19, 20, **21**, 22, 23: *falcata* **15**, **16**, 20, **20**; *gladius Hispaniensis* **10**, **12**, 17, **17**, 20, 22, 35, **35**, 59, **66–67**; *kopis* 15, 20

Ticinus, battle of (218 BC) 29, 58, 76
Trebia, battle of the (216 BC) **10**, 29–30, 34, 41, 49, 58, 76
triarii 16, 17, 18, 27, **27**, 34, 37, 48
tribunes 26, 36, 55, 56

Upper Baetis, battle of the (211 BC) 58, 74

velites 17, 18, 27, **27**, 45, 64
  use in combat 34, **47**, 48, 49, 50, 55, 60, **61**, **66–67**, 68, 69–70

Zama, battle of (202 BC) 5, 62, 77